D1130677

Michel Tournier

Twayne's World Authors Series

French Literature

David O'Connell, Editor

University of Illinois

TWAS 747

MICHEL TOURNIER
(1924–   )
Photograph courtesy of
Jacques Robert, N.R.F.

Michel Tournier

By William Cloonan

Florida State University

Twayne Publishers • *Boston*

Michel Tournier

William Cloonan

Copyright © 1985 by G. K. Hall & Company
All Rights Reserved
Published by Twayne Publishers
A Division of G. K. Hall & Co.
A publishing subsidiary of ITT
70 Lincoln Street
Boston, Massachusetts 02111

Book Production by Elizabeth Todesco
Book Design by Barbara Anderson

Printed on permanent/durable acid-free
paper and bound in the United States of
America.

Library of Congress Cataloging in Publication Data

Cloonan, William J.
  Michel Tournier.

  (Twayne's world authors series; TWAS 747)
  Bibliography: p. 107
  Includes index.
  1. Tournier, Michel—Criticism and interpretation.
I. Title. II. Series.
PQ2680.O83Z65 1985   843'.914   84–22403
ISBN 0–8057–6595–6

To Deborah

Contents

About the Author

William Cloonan holds a doctorate in comparative literature from the University of North Carolina at Chapel Hill. His fields of interest include seventeenth-century French drama and the twentieth-century American and European novel. He has published articles on seventeenth-century topics as well as one book-length study, *Racine's Theatre: The Politics of Love* (1978). He has written articles on twentieth-century novelists for both scholarly journals and the *New Boston Review*.

Preface

In February 1983 the French minister of culture, Jack Lang, organized an international conference that purported to examine the relationship between politics and the arts. While Lang was well-pleased with his efforts, many observers thought otherwise. This conference was the object of much ridicule in the press, whose choruses of disapproval tended to vary only in the degree of sarcasm expended. Raymond Sokolov of the *Wall Street Journal* wrote a particularly controversial article that decried what he took to be the pervasive sterility of contemporary French culture. Yet amid his generally gloomy view of the state of the arts in France, Sokolov did note one isolated example of excellence: "France has produced no writers of real importance in twenty years, except for Michel Tournier."[1]

Michel Tournier has yet to become the subject of extensive academic criticism, but he is extremely popular among educated, well-read people. Part of the reason for this has to do with what he is not. Tournier is not "un nouveau romancier" ("a new novelist"). His novels have clearly articulated plots and readily discernible beginnings, middles, and ends. Except for his critical essays, he says practically nothing about the agony of artistic creation or the intricacies of currently fashionable psychoanalytical theories. If he has read Lacan, Foucault, Derrida, or Barthes, it is not immediately evident in his writings. What Tournier does write about are the crises that have perplexed and fascinated his contemporaries: the shattering moral and philosophical implications of World War II, the ambiguity of sexual identity, the desire to find some means of ordering experience in the midst of the chaos of the modern world, and the role that fiction plays in the unfolding of daily life. (Tournier is also a photographer of merit and has written extensively on the subject, but this aspect of his talent will only figure in the present study to the extent it impinges upon his literary creation.)

Michel Tournier is a popular novelist, an expression that is often used condescendingly, but which here means nothing other than that he writes about matters of general human concern. He does not, however, do this simplistically. The novels' accessibility facilitates a reader's entry into the author's fictional universe, but what lies within challenges many commonly held assumptions about life's meaning and goals. Tournier writes nineteenth-century novels about twentieth-century experiences.

This study will assess Tournier's fictional and critical writings in terms of the issues they raise and the myths they articulate as a means of clarifying the contemporary situation. The first chapter will discuss Tournier's life and times with special consideration given to his views about literature. The bases of this analysis will be his autobiographical essay, *Le Vent Paraclet* (The holy spirit) and his collection of essays, *Le Vol du vampire* (The flight of the vampire). The following chapters will focus on Tournier's novels and study each one in detail. The section that deals with his collection of shorter pieces, *Le Coq de bruyère* (The grouse) will show how these minor works reflect the same concerns as the novels.

Most of Tournier's major writings have been translated into English and a list of the translations will appear in the bibliography, but I shall use my own translations throughout the book.

William Cloonan

Florida State University

Chronology

Chapter One

Michel Tournier and His World

The Image and the Man

On the first page of *Le Vent Paraclet* Michel Tournier describes an event in the early life of his maternal grandfather. Edouard Tournier was six years old in 1871 when the triumphant Prussians marched into his little village of Bligny-sur-Ouche. The head of the military band chose the reluctant Edouard to carry a bulky score during the victory parade. Humiliated as only a child patriot can be, his head hidden behind the sheet music, Edouard sobbed uncontrollably as he staggered down the street.[1]

This image of the sensitive young man who protects his emotions behind what may loosely be qualified as a work of art invites comparison with Tournier himself. The author even implies as much: "A child in tears, hidden behind the book he carries, this little image that has become traditional in the family can serve as a frontispiece for this essay" (*VP*, 9). Yet this image is totally misleading. Tournier, as his numerous photographic self-portraits and interviews in print and on radio and television indicate, is not one to hide his thoughts and feelings. He is always in evidence, albeit to the side of his works, and constantly smiling.

In another sense, however, this deliberately melodramatic description of Edouard does suggest two important characteristics of Tournier the man and the artist: his skill with irony and his delight in masks. André Malraux's greatest fictional creation was certainly himself, and his finest novel the supposed autobiography, *Antimémoires*. It is a tribute to Tournier that the fiction of his novels far surpasses the fabulation that he spins around himself, but it is nevertheless useful to realize that the Michel Tournier who presents himself in countless public forums is also something of a literary creation. What makes Tournier's ironic self-fictionalizations significant is that the most remarkable theme of his writings, more startling in a way than his treatment of myth, twinship, and sexual identity, is his insistence that the traditional distinction between truth and fiction is largely nonexistent. What human beings perceive as reality is the product of innumerable, unconscious manipulations of the chaos about them, manipulations that seek to impose an order and coherence onto a world that most often lacks both. If there is any purely utilitarian aspect to Tournier's work, it is to invite people to appreciate, and even enjoy, the enormous role that fiction plays in the unfolding of their daily lives.

The best way to understand his autobiographical essay, *Le Vent Paraclet,* as well as the occasional personal revelations that appear in his collection of essays, *Le Vol du vampire,* is for the reader to accept that he is participating in the author's self-creation, that Michel Tournier is doing consciously and within the confines of several hundred pages, what others do unthinkingly throughout the course of their lives.

The "facts" of Tournier's life are readily available. Born in Paris in 1924, he was of the generation that was slightly too young to engage in World War II. But by dint of living in Paris and Saint Germain-en-Laye (a Parisian suburb) during the conflict, Tournier was able to experience the reality of the Occupation. He witnessed the hunger and the humiliation, but also the admiration of many French people for their German conquerors as well as their mindless confidence in Pétain and the Vichy government. And at the war's end he observed how all these events were rapidly fictionalized and transformed into the myth of "La France résistante." Michel Tournier did not have to await Marcel Ophuls' superb film, *Le Chagrin et la Pitié* (*The Sorrow and the Pity*) to learn that the French Resistance was the work of an often despised minority whose activities were usually as inefficient as they were heroic.

Perhaps more than most of the French, Tournier was aware of the horror of national hatreds since his family was as much pro-German as it was anti-Nazi. His mother and father spoke German and he himself had spent many summers in Germany. Tournier is one of the rare modern French writers—Jean Giraudoux is the only other who comes quickly to mind—who genuinely appreciates the language and culture of the people who live on the other side of the Rhine.

Shortly after the end of the war, Tournier set out for what was to be a brief sojourn at the German University of Tübingen where he intended to study philosophy. This short visit lasted four years. Upon his return to Paris, he set about preparing for the *agrégation* (a sort of doctorate earned through a series of difficult exams but which does not include a dissertation in the American sense of the word). Tournier mentions in passing in *Le Vent Paraclet* that at the time he considered himself the best philosopher of his generation (*VP*, 158). To his complete astonishment he failed the exam, and as a result he abandoned all hope for a career as an academic philosopher. Tournier then began to work as an editor for a Parisian publishing house and as a translator of German works. With regard to this latter activity, Tournier is probably best known for his translations of Erich Maria Remarque. Gradually he drifted into the radio industry where he was an announcer for Europe Number 1 (the influence of this experience appears in his short story, "Tristan Vox," in the collection, *Le Coq de bruyère*). With the advent of television Tournier turned his attention to that medium.

Michel Tournier was to all appearances well established as a middle-brow intellectual when, at the age of forty-three, he published *Vendredi, ou les limbes du Pacifique* (*Friday, or the Other Island*), the first in a series of astonishing novels. This work won for the fledgling author the prestigious Grand Prix du Roman de l'Académie Française (the Grand Prize for Fiction from the French Academy). With the publication of *Le Roi des Aulnes* (*The Ogre*) in 1970, which won him the Prix Goncourt and later an invitation to join the Académie Goncourt, Tournier established himself as one of France's leading contemporary novelists.

As any reader of Tournier will rapidly learn, he lives in a former rectory, situated in the valley of the Chevreuse where, surrounded by his photographs, his garden, and frequently visited by the local children, he manages to observe the activities of his fellow creatures while maintaining a certain distance from them. To employ an expression from Albert Camus's short story,

"Jonas, ou l'artiste au travail" (Jonas, or the artist at work),
Michel Tournier is at once "solidaire" and "solitaire" ("united"
and "isolated") with respect to the world about him.

The events selected in this biographical sketch have implications for Tournier's writing. Germany is for him a mythic domain and myth plays a central role in all his novels; his long
period of reflection and development before publishing has
given Tournier some pronounced views about fiction writing
and literature in general; his philosophic interests affect everything he writes, and his carefully sculpted *persona* attests to the
importance that Tournier gives to creation, both in literature
and life. The remainder of this chapter will develop these themes
which play significant roles in his writings.

Myth

For Michel Tournier a myth is, on its simplest level, a fundamental story (*VP*, 183)—one that every human being already
knows. Thus to read a myth is actually to reread it, since the
reader encounters on the page something he already possesses
in some recess of his mind. In *Le Vent Paraclet* Tournier mentions
that André Gide claimed that he wrote not to be read, but to
be reread, the second reading apparently being the important
one for Gide (*VP*, 184). Tournier amends this statement in a
way that shows how powerful he considers myths to be: "My
books should be recognized—reread—at the first reading" (*VP*,
187).

There are many complicated explanations for the origins of
myth, but the only one that concerns Tournier involves the
influence of literature. He insists upon literature's role in the
creation of mythic prototypes. Tournier is convinced that Rousseau "invented" the beauty of mountains for generations to
come (*VP*, 187) and that Goethe's *Werther* changed the way
that people love: "It is true today that nobody would love the
way he does if Goethe had not written *Werther*" (*VP*, 188).
In *Le Vol du vampire* Tournier provides a brilliant and imaginative defense of his thesis about *Werther,* and he does so while
scarcely using a word of his own. In an essay entitled "Kleist
ou la mort d'un poète: Dossier" (Kleist or the death of a poet:
documents), Tournier quotes with only the barest historical com-

mentary the letters of Heinrich Kleist and Henriette Vogel to their friends in the days that preceded their mutual suicide. These letters resemble Werther's correspondence to an astonishing degree. They express the same sort of latent cruelty to others that suffuses Werther's writing, as well as the fascination with oblivion that prefigures Wagner's *Liebestod*. Whether or not, as Tournier says, "romanticism was the grave-digger of wisdom" (*VP*, 275), the Kleist-Vogel correspondence definitely illustrates how greatly life is formed by art.

The letters of Kleist and Vogel written, as it were, under the shadow of Werther, demonstrate Tournier's contention that the underlying function of myth is to celebrate human beings' inability and unwillingness to adapt themselves to society: "The adulterous passion of Tristan and Isolde, Faust's pact with the devil, the destructive desire of Don Juan, the fierce solitude of Robinson Crusoe, and the extravagant dream of Don Quixote are so many ways of saying 'no' to society, of breaking down the social order."[2] Myth for Tournier has nothing to do with social integration; it is a reminder of life's disorder ("un rappel au désordre" [*V*, 32]) and, as such, a celebration of the outcast, the nay-sayer. In a different context Tournier suggests that the notorious anti-Semitism of the great novelist Celine was his way of saying "shit to mankind" ("une façon de dire merde à toute humanité" [*V*, 249]). Substitute "society" for "mankind" and one can say that a comparable sentiment animates the myths that Tournier believes to be the most powerful in Western culture.

Tournier thinks that some myths are essentially feminine and others masculine. Don Juan is the male myth par excellence, while Tristan is a female myth: "Don Juan dominates and scorns a vast herd of women. . . . Tristan is the prey of a troop of women who allow him no means of escape" (*V*, 33). Yet, whether male or female, myths constitute a rejection of socially acceptable canons of behavior and a longing for a degree of emotional intensity that "civilized" society has learned to repress.

The writer's function, according to Tournier, is to renew the myths that "form the substance of his contemporaries' souls" (*V*, 390). Myth is for him mortal; it can die and there is even a name for a dead myth: allegory. Allegory is the "mummy of a great idea which lacks a creative genius to give it new life" (*V,* 390). Myths abound in Tournier's novels, but there is one mythic structure that dominates his work. That is the myth of twinship.

Tournier associates the myth of twinship with two types of opposing yet complimentary human personalities. One is the sedentary, the person who fears the complex and unforeseen and hopes to have his life unfold in a totally predictable manner within a clearly demarcated geographical space. The other is the nomad, the individual who, at times despite himself, becomes a wanderer and finds himself forced to confront some of life's uncertainties. These two descriptions conform nicely to the biblical myth of Cain and Abel. Cain is the farmer, the man whose life is contained within the parameters of his fields, while his brother Abel is a shepherd, constantly on the move in search of new grazing areas. Associated with these two personality types are two kinds of time. Clock time ("temps de l'horloge") is preferred by the Cains since it bespeaks the careful regulation and control of every moment of human existence. The alternative is meteoric time ("temps des météores") which reflects human experience in all its disorder.

It is tempting to divide Tournier's characters into Cains and Abels. For example, one might say that the Robinson of *Vendredi* is a Cain for much of the novel and the slave Vendredi is an Abel. In *Le Roi des Aulnes* the conveniently named Abel Tiffauges would be an Abel, and his friend Nestor, who never leaves the schoolyard, is a Cain. The globe-trotting Jean in *Les Météores* would be an Abel and his brother Paul, a Cain.

Despite the convenience of this schema, it simply does not work. No single character is totally a Cain or an Abel; each has within himself the potential to be the other. In "La famille Adam" (Adam's family), the first story in the collection *Le Coq de bruyère,* Cain becomes both the hero and the wanderer; at certain moments in *Le Roi des Aulnes* Abel displays the characteristics of Nestor/Cain, and in *Les Météores* the sedentary Paul travels around the world in pursuit of his brother. What the myth of twinship indicates for Tournier is that the quest for self-fulfillment involves a struggle, not only with the beloved and despised other, but within the individual himself.

There also exists a hierarchy of twinship. The Abels and

Nestors and the Robinsons and Vendredis are imperfect twins. While they complement each other, they are obviously born of different seeds and have different physiques. Thus their unions, whether intellectual, emotional, or physical, will always be imperfect. The true twins are the perfect twins, the couple born of the same seed and who have an exact resemblance. These couples are rare (one such has a minor role in *Le Roi des Aulnes*), but it is the twins Jean and Paul, so perfectly alike that they are commonly referred to as Jean-Paul, that best illustrate the significance of the perfect twin. This complicated issue will be discussed in the chapter on *Les Météores,* but for the moment suffice it to say that their perfection is replete with dangers for them.

Tournier and the Contemporary French Novel

Tournier's ironic humor emerges when he describes both how he came to be a novelist and the sort of novelist he is: "I wanted to be the Hegel of my generation, but am instead the Huysmans."[3] Tournier frequently insists that his path to literature is atypical of that of his contemporaries, yet it is certainly no different from that of Jean-Paul Sartre, a man he admired greatly. Sartre also had to "find a passage between philosophy and the novel."[4] While neither man ever denied his philosophic interests, both Tournier and the Sartre of *Nausea* and *The Age of Reason* proved capable of writing fiction that was considerably more complex than "un roman à thèse" ("thesis novel"). In an interview, Tournier maintained that he had never created a character who was "un cas général" ("a type character"),[5] and this despite his fascination with mythic figures.

What makes Tournier stand out among his contemporaries is not his academic background. Rather, he is one of the few novelists in France today (Marguerite Yourcenar is another) who writes serious novels that achieve widespread popularity. One explanation for this is Tournier's avoidance of techniques associated with the *nouveau roman* ("new novel"). Tournier describes himself as a writer of "traditional novels" (*VP,* 189), and, in what one assumes is the artist's joke at the expense of the critics, he cites as his models a collection of popular second-rate authors such as Paul Bourget and René Bazin (*VP,* 189).

Tournier has always insisted that, unlike the *nouveaux romanciers,* he has no interest in attempting to renew the form of the novel. Instead, he wants "to express in a traditional, safe, and reassuring form a content that possesses none of these qualities" (*VP,* 190). To illustrate what he means by this, Tournier repeats a story that concerns the composers Erik Satie and Maurice Ravel. When Ravel was offered the Légion d'honneur (Legion of Honor) by the French government, he turned it down. Satie remarked that Ravel might well have refused this sign of middle-class approbation, but all his music accepted it. When Tournier himself received the Légion d'honneur, he accepted it without a qualm, but then noted that "I can accept the Légion d'honneur because all my work rejects it."[6]

In *Le Vent Paraclet* Tournier says that Paul Valéry's *Monsieur Teste* has provided him with the definition of and model for all the books he has wanted to write (*VP,* 223). He explains that "In *Monsieur Teste* Valéry endows an imaginary personage with an extraordinary mentality and then he releases him in the world and observes the result" (*VP,* 225). In *Le Vol du vampire* Tournier elaborates his notion of the artist's function: "To regard without doing anything, to see all while touching nothing, this is the condition of the novelist" (*V,* 266). Now such a highly intellectualized formulation of the novelist's task is typical of many modernist and postmodernist artists, and as such it reveals little about how a particular author actually works. Tournier tells more about his personal artistic ambitions and interests when he describes more specifically what he does in his novels. He admits that there are some autobiographical elements in his books, but denies that they are particularly significant (*VP,* 102). On the contrary, he insists that a true novel must be peopled with numerous characters different from one another and from the author. He cites as examples of novelists who do this successfully Balzac, Hugo, and, appearances to the contrary, Proust (*V,* 213).

Tournier divides fiction into three categories, "la nouvelle" ("the nouvella"), "la fable" ("the fable"), and "le conte" ("the story"). "La nouvelle" is faithful to everyday life and is characterized by what Tournier calls a strict and gray realism (*V,* 36). Maupassant, Chekhov, and Sartre are examples of authors who write *nouvelles.* What distinguishes "la fable" is its insistence upon offering a little moralizing lesson at the end and La Fontaine is the obvious example. Midway between "la nouvelle" and "la fable" is "le conte" and this is Tournier's territory. "Le conte" does more than describe quotidian experience, since the story's significance goes beyond the limitations of the events described. However, this significance, unlike that of "la fable," is not immediately apparent: "the story presents itself as a translucid but not transparent milieu, a glaucous density wherein the reader sees emerging figures that he cannot quite completely grasp . . . the story is a haunted nouvella, haunted by a spectral significance that touches us, enriches us, but does not instruct us" (*V,* 37). Tournier's own preference is clear; in a radio interview he plainly stated: "I only write *contes.*"[7]

Shortly after Tournier published his 1980 novel, *Gaspard, Melchior et Balthazar* (*The Four Wise Men*), he began to refer to his style of writing as similar to Huysmans's "naturalisme mystique" ("mystical naturalism"). Tournier's relationship to Huysmans and religion in general will be discussed in the chapter on *Gaspard, Melchior et Balthazar,* but for the nonce it can be said that this rather striking formulation, "naturalisme mystique," is only a more elaborate way of adverting to what Tournier understands by a *conte.* The essential qualities remain the same. However exotic the setting, great attention is devoted to historical and geographical detail. (Much like Flaubert, Tournier is a patient and gifted researcher.) Nevertheless, elements in the story move the reader out of the realm of the purely historical novel and into a world of fascinating ambiguity that defies simplistic explanation. Whatever Tournier chooses to call his fiction, his novels have no set meaning, but many possible interpretations.

The question of interpretation leads to an interesting aspect of Tournier's ideas about literature. He ascribes great importance to the reader's participation in literary creation. For him, the reader is "the author's indispensable collaborator" (*V,* 10); so much so that a book that is written but not read does not completely exist (*V,* 10). It is the reader who is free to interpret the book, and in this domain his liberty is absolute: "a novel can have a thesis, but only provided that it is the reader, not the author, who puts it there."[8] If it is the novelist who creates the characters, it is, according to Tournier, the reader's imagination that brings them to life, and from this perspective "the criterion of a masterpiece is easy to define: it is the participation in the joy of creation that the book offers the reader" (*V*, 19). With regard to his own reading, Tournier suggests a means of determining whether a work possesses genius, and the criteria he mentions might be applied to his own novels as well: "I consider works to be inspired [*géniales*] by virtue of the effect of expansion, deepening, enrichment, and liberation that they have on my current vision of the world" (*V*, 24).

Tournier and Philosophy

Michel Tournier makes much of his background in philosophy. Indeed, he insists so frequently upon it and makes such extensive claims for its influence on his writing, that it becomes at times difficult not to suspect irony: "I have the ambition to furnish my readers who are avid for love and adventure the literary equivalent of those sublime metaphysical inventions such as Descartes's *cogito,* Spinoza's three types of knowledge, Leibniz's pre-established harmonies, Kant's transcendental schematism, Husserl's phenomenological reduction, to cite several major models" (*VP,* 175). A comparable assertion in *Le Vol du vampire* is only slightly less hyperbolic: "I have never published anything that did not derive secretly and indirectly from Plato, Aristotle, Spinoza, Leibniz, and several others" (*V,* 382).

It is doubtless true that Sartre's *Being and Nothingness* had a great influence on the young Tournier (*VP,* 155), that Plato's *Symposium* is one source of Tournier's ideas about twinship, that the three stages Robinson goes through in *Vendredi* do, in a sense, correspond to the three types of knowledge Spinoza describes in his *Ethics* (*VP,* 328), and that the title for *Les Météores* comes from Aristotle's *The Meteors.* Yet the question of influence is always an elusive subject, one that is best approached gingerly. For example, the title *Les Météores* brings Aristotle to mind, but the novel's first pages are obviously a parody of Robert Musil's *Der Mann ohne Eigenschaften* (*The Man Without Qualities*). Concerning his titles it is quite possible that Tournier is merely playing with literary allusions whose real significance is slight.

The difficulties of ascribing influence are compounded when one enters into the realm of ideas which is "philosophy." Whatever the elements that constitute a novel, the finished product is something other than the sum of its ideas, and the imaginative quality of literature has been known to force curious transformations upon the philosophic speculations that contribute to a work of fiction. Thomas Mann's *The Magic Mountain* and Hesse's *Magister Ludi,* two novels that Tournier admires, offer good examples of philosophic concepts made to run amok in the interest of literary effect.

If, then, one has a certain hesitancy to ascribe anything resembling a perfect linkage between philosophy and fiction in Tournier's novels, there nevertheless remains an area where Tournier's philosophic interests are both evident and useful to the student of literature.

Tournier's literary criticism displays his philosophic training, especially with regard to categorization. Tournier divides the major French writers into two groups, *primaires* ("primaries") and *sécondaires* ("secondaries"); he uses a concept called "le rire blanc" ("white laughter") to elucidate other authors' works and by extension his own as well; and, finally, in a discussion of the literary implication of heredity and environment he makes a suggestion that will prove extremely valuable for the understanding of his own fiction.

The difference between the primaries and the secondaries is supposed to have nothing to do with the literary merit of the authors' works. It has to do with their attitude toward life. The primaries are those who affirm a joy in human existence, who proclaim an emphatic "yes" to life. The primary is fascinated by youth and the eternal present (*V,* 227). For Tournier, André Gide is the best example of this category; when he speaks of Gide's talent for focusing only upon the positive aspects of the Bible, he remarks: "All of Gide's works will have consisted of tearing the Scriptures from the fir trees to give them to the palms" (*V,* 232). Other primaries would include Voltaire, Colette, and Théophile Gauthier.

A secondary "lives in constant reference to his past and his future. The nostalgia for what no longer exists and the fear of what is going to happen darken his present and undercut his immediate sensations. His intelligence employs calculation rather than intuition. . . . In love fidelity outweighs liberty" (*V,* 227). Examples of this group would include Valéry, Rous-

seau, Baudelaire, and Sartre. The most terrifying of the secondaries are Proust and Céline whose work reflect an intense
hatred of life (*V,* 249). Yet in *Vol du vampire* Tournier asserts
that Proust and Céline are also the two greatest French authors
of the century (*V,* 302), and in an interview, he adds a third,
Sartre.[9]

Can one place Tournier within either of these categories?
The answer to this question involves a discussion of white laughter.

In *Le Vent Paraclet* Tournier mentions that Gaston Bachelard
revealed to him that a fundamental aspect of philosophy was
laughter (*VP,* 148), and that the approach to the absolute is
indicated by laughter (*VP,* 149). However, the particular laughter that Tournier has in mind is special. The person who experiences white laughter has just "glimpsed the abyss yawning
between the loosened stitches of things. He suddenly knows
that nothing matters. He is seized by anguish, but then by white
laughter delivered from all fear . . . when the weakened planks
of a footbridge open onto total nothingness, most men do not
see anything, but some see the nothingness. These people look
without trembling at their feet and happily sing that the king
is naked. White laughter is their rallying cry" (*VP,* 194). White
laughter denounces the "transient, relative" nature of things
(*VP,* 193).

White laughter reflects an awareness of life's utter meaninglessness, a meaninglessness so complete that it goes beyond tragedy; the only possible response to this experience is laughter.
It is an articulation of white laughter that Tournier finds in
Thomas Mann's enigmatic statement: "the more I laugh, the
less I am joking" (*V,* 291).

White laughter connotes a respect for truth in all its terror.
Yet it is not an act of total negation. To experience white laughter is to accept that if any sense be ascribed to existence it
will necessarily be artificial and invented by human beings. Thus
to discover a meaning in things is to create and then participate
in an elaborate and often quite enjoyable game.

It is possible to compare Tournier's idea of white laughter
with certain aspects of Camus's interpretation of the Myth of
Sisyphus. Camus's absurd hero and the person who knows white
laughter have both grasped life's senselessness, yet each contin-

ues to seek a means not just of living, but of living happily. The difference is that whereas Camus envisions happiness as the result, at least in part, of the struggle along with and for other people, Tournier describes the experience of white laughter as one of absolute isolation. His characters who have encountered white laughter attempt to wrest pleasure out of people and events by any means possible. If white laughter has any moral or social function, it is to justify total egocentricity.

White laughter suffuses artistic creation. The artist imposes an order upon life's meaninglessness, but how much or even whether this order corresponds to reality cannot ever be known. Thus the ensuing art work is replete with ambiguity; it deceives as much as it pleases since its aim is to provide a structure to human experience that must necessarily be artificial.

An appreciation of white laughter is crucial to an understanding of Tournier's use of myth. The artist creates an order whose beauty masks its artificiality. Myths are a source of order and beauty, but it should be recalled that for Tournier myth does not spring from some collective unconscious; it has its origins in the mind of the artist and therefore *might* be nothing other than enticing illusion.

To return to the categories of primary and secondary authors, there are two conclusions to draw. If by "better writer" one means an artist who grapples with more levels of complexity, whose vision of the world is more troubling and elusive than those of his fellows, then the secondaries are clearly superior to the primaries. It is not due to the vagaries of personal taste that Tournier values the works of Céline, Proust, and Sartre so highly. In his terms, all three have undergone and expressed the experience of white laughter. The second conclusion is that Michel Tournier, whose interviews and essays attest to his love of life and delight in the present, is nonetheless in terms of his artistic creation, permeated as it is by white laughter, a secondary.

Tournier's treatment of heredity and environment illuminates an important aspect of his own creative activity. For him the argument concerning whether heredity or environment is the predominant influence on an individual's development has implications for literature. Tournier believes, for example, that characters in Racine and Balzac are essentially indifferent to their

milieu; what animates them comes from within and exterior
circumstances function merely as catalysts for the unfolding
of inevitable destinies. Tournier contrasts these authors with
Corneille and Hugo whose characters are victims of their envi-
ronments, men and women who react to fortuitous events and
thus create situations that might have been avoided.

What matters here is not the objective strength or weakness
of Tournier's distinctions, but the way they can be applied to
his own work. Tournier describes "destiny" in the following
terms: "It is appropriate to speak of destiny when the things
which happen to me, the things which make and unmake my
life, betray a superior logic, an intelligible necessity that is only
partially clear to me" (*VP*, 233). Tournier's view of destiny
is similar to his understanding of heredity. Certainly it would
appear that at first glance his main characters act in accordance
with some dimly perceived logic and consider themselves to
be fulfilling some preordained role. In *Le Roi des Aulnes* Abel
Tiffauges's statement that "I also believe that I have emerged
from the night of time"[10] reflects a belief common to most of
Tournier's heroes. It is the utter certainty of living a destined
existence that provides these characters with what is at least
the appearance of great strength.

Tournier's conception of the function of heredity and environment ultimately becomes more nuanced than a clash of opposites.
In *Vol du vampire* he remarks that "one would not be giving
a false idea of the relation between heredity and environment
to say that the flowering of the human personality is a conquest
of environment over heredity, of the constructed over the given,
of liberty over fate" (*V*, 148–49). In his novels, which on first
reading seem to accord such great importance to the acting
out of an inevitable destiny, there is always the possibility that
these characters are just fooling themselves, that their strength
is nothing other than a determination not to develop, not to
see themselves and their milieu clearly. Abel, Paul, and even
Robinson might be victims of a narrowly conceived self-image.
No reader of Michel Tournier can afford to forget that behind
these characters' discussions of fate, destiny, perfect twinship,
and deciphering grids, there is a clever artist who knows what
is meant by white laughter.

The Vicar of the Chevreuse

In Tournier's expository writing he cites numerous authors who have influenced him (Valéry, Spinoza, Plato) or whom he personally admires (Gide, Colette). While one can question the importance of the role that some of these figures played in Tournier's development, there is one person whose influence on Tournier the individual and the artist is incontestable: Jean-Jacques Rousseau. The resemblances between these two men are striking. Rousseau's philosophic interests, his preference for the country over the city, his love for children (at least in theory) and need for solitude all find their echoes in Tournier. The vicar of Savoy has his twentieth-century embodiment in the vicar of the Chevreuse.

Rousseau and Tournier share a tendency to score a point through a reversal of a cliché and then an exaggeration of the reversal. As Rousseau noted: "Do the opposite of the expected, and you will almost always do the right thing."[11] If for no other reason, Tournier will always be famous in France for his casual remark in *Le Vent Paraclet* that it was a pity that the Germans did not burn down Paris during the War (*VP*, 82). What Tournier was actually discussing was the coldness of the modern city, and he chose a means of expressing his thoughts that would not go unnoticed. Yet listen to Rousseau on the same subject: "France would be much more powerful if Paris were destroyed."[12] Indeed, Rousseau proved himself more courageous than Tournier when he decided to confront the twin sources of France's greatest pride: "The French do not know how to eat since it requires a special art to make their food palatable,"[13] and "the French language is the most obscene."[14]

Rousseau and Tournier both revel in the role of gadflies, and their writings display an impatience with social conformity and mores. Rousseau's assertion that all is folly and contradiction in human institutions is demonstrated throughout Tournier's fiction. Rousseau responded to the increasing sophistication of eighteenth-century life by championing a more simplified lifestyle and a respect for cultural diversity. Tournier's impassioned defense of the Third World shows both his hatred for racism and his awareness of the corrupting influence of Western indus-

trial society. It is hardly surprising that two such keen observers
of their respective epochs, men who judged the word "progress"
to be most often misused, would each be drawn to Robinson
Crusoe.

Chapter Two

Vendredi, ou les limbes du Pacifique

Two Novels

In *Emile,* Rousseau announced that while he hated books (they only teach people to talk about things they do not understand),[1] there was one book he would permit his imaginary pupil to read: *Robinson Crusoe* by Daniel Defoe. According to Rousseau, "the surest means of raising Emile above prejudices and focusing his judgment on the true relations between things is to put him in the place of an isolated man and then to judge everything as this man would, namely with regard to the utility of things."[2] Tournier shares Rousseau's respect for *Robinson Crusoe,* although his understanding of "utility" will not be confined to practical matters.

The titles of all Tournier's novels reflect the influence of some literary predecessor. The expression "le roi des aulnes" is the French translation of the German "der Erlkönig," and immediately calls to mind Goethe's famous poem. The title *Les Météores* conjures up Aristotle's *The Meteors,* and *Gaspard, Melchior et Balthazar* are the names ascribed to the biblical Magi who made the journey to Bethlehem. Yet of all Tournier's novels, it is only *Vendredi* that warrants extensive comparison with its alleged model. In a loose fashion *Vendredi* follows Defoe's story line for about two thirds of the way, and the similarities and differences between the eighteenth- and twentieth-century versions of Crusoe's travails help clarify Tournier's aims and accomplishments in this, his first novel.

Vendredi

Vendredi begins aboard ship. The exact date is 29 September 1759. To pass the time during a severe storm Captain Pieter

Van Deyssel is reading Robinson's fortune in the tarot cards. He discovers, or claims to discover, that Robinson is essentially an organizer, a pers. who functions best in a carefully controlled environment. ' ~ard that indicates this is "le bateleur" ("buffon," "mountebar and Van Deyssel adds that the organizing activities of "le ba r" are illusory, although he does not know that since "skepu is not his forte."[3] The captain says that Robinson is of th that never doubts anything, that he lives in a world of c. ies. Robinson's destiny will nevertheless be difficult and i. ught with danger, yet in the end he will be saved by a child who will emerge from the earth's entrails and present him with the keys to the City of the Sun. Before Robinson can question Van Deyssel further, the ship experiences a violent shock and begins to break apart. Water sweeps everything away.

When Robinson awakens he is alone on an island. His initial reaction is the same as Defoe's Crusoe: out of solitude and despair he christens the island "Desolation." As Robinson explores his island/prison he has the vague sense that its geography resembles the contours of a human body, but he does not dwell on this curious intuition. He begins instead to plot his escape and starts building a boat he calls *Evasion*. Robinson makes the same mistake as did Defoe's Crusoe. He finishes the boat after considerable labor, but only to discover that he has no way of getting it into the water. His ambition has exceeded ability.

Disgusted with himself, Robinson sinks into a stagnant pool, "la souille," whose filthy waters teem with fungi, insects, and leeches. In each of his subsequent depressions, Robinson will return to this place.

Robinson finally drags himself out of "la souille" and resolves to make the best of his lot. He renames the island "Speranza" ("Hope"), in an effort to put matters in a more positive light. Robinson now remarks that the island has the form of a woman's body.

Slowly he begins to cultivate the land, raise flocks of sheep, and generally try to impose a civilized, Western order onto his tropical habitat. Like Defoe's hero, some of Robinson's "improvements" border on the insane. He conquers his loathing for the vultures who follow him everywhere by ordaining that they comprise the island's administrative council, and when he builds a modest church he decrees that the right side is reserved for women (there are not any). Nonetheless, he is happy with his work and when he manages to tame the ship's dog Tenn, who had fled him earlier when he was constructing the ill-fated *Evasion,* he convinces himself that he is making progress.

Over the years of solitude Robinson maintains a fragile mental equilibrium. More than anything else, work sustains him, even though his accomplishments far surpass his needs. He builds rice patties, canals, and bridges and eventually stores up more food than he could consume in a lifetime. He constructs a water clock, establishes laws for governing the island ("urination and defecation can only take place in prescribed areas" [*Ve,* 62]), and establishes a Conservatory of Weights and Measures (*Ve,* 59). Robinson's obsession with order is behind all these improvements.

One day he discovers a cave that leads to what he takes to be Speranza's womb. When he spends time there, the clock stops and the daily self-imposed tasks remain undone. Still, his time in Speranza's womb provides his only pleasure. This joy proves, however, to be short-lived. Robinson discovers that when he enters the cave and Speranza is, so to speak, full with him, the island loses its fertility and the goats give no milk. Regretfully, he spaces his visits at longer and longer intervals.

Although Defoe's Crusoe was anxious to rescue Friday and thereby have a slave, Tournier's Robinson does not choose to save Vendredi. He intended to shoot the boy as he was fleeing his captives because he did not want the cannibals to explore the island and possibly discover his whereabouts. It was Tenn whose nervousness disrupted Robinson's aim and the bullet meant for Vendredi struck one of his pursuers.

Vendredi proves to be docile and obedient, but totally indifferent to the progress that Robinson has made on the island. One day Vendredi inadvertently throws a lighted pipe into a part of Speranza's cave where the gunpowder was hidden and Robinson's laboriously ordered universe literally explodes under him.

When Robinson has his second awakening on the island he discovers his meticulously ordered world in shambles and his dog, Tenn, dead. The dog, traditionally Western man's best

friend, is an ironic symbol for the civilized social values that
have now been destroyed. Robinson greets their demise with
relief. He no longer struggles against his natural surroundings,
but, taking Vendredi as his guide, begins to enjoy them.

Robinson begins to live like a savage. He no longer wears
clothing and follows with awe and fascination Vendredi's struggles with a gigantic ram, Andaor. From the ram's hide the boy
makes a kite and he turns Andaor's skull into the equivalent
of an Aeolian harp. Robinson starts to discover the true Speranza, the hidden island, and Vendredi comes to represent for
him the aerial, celestial soul whose openness to life in its myriad
forms contrasts with his own plodding, earth-bound being. At
this point Robinson prays to the Sun to make him more like
Vendredi (*Ve,* 175).

After years of exploring his new sense of himself, Robinson's
self-examinations are interrupted by the arrival of a British ship.
Vendredi is intrigued by all that is Western and modern, while
Robinson is appalled by the ship's captain's stories of wars that
breed more wars. Robinson is also taken aback by the British
sailors' indifference to nature and their acquisitiveness, traits
that characterized his earlier years on Speranza. He decides to
stay on the island but when the ship leaves he is horrified to
realize that Vendredi has departed with it. On the verge of
what would be his final despair, Robinson finds in Speranza's
cave the cabinboy who had jumped ship. Van Deyssel's predic-
tion, that Robinson would be saved by a child, appears to have
come true, and the joyous Robinson rechristens the boy Thurs-
day, which is "the Sunday of children" (*Ve,* 205).

Defoe's Crusoe and Tournier's Robinson

The most obvious difference between Defoe's *Robinson Crusoe*
and Tournier's *Vendredi ou les limbes du Pacifique* is their respective
titles. Both novels deal with the same characters and situations,
but what distinguishes them, even more than differences of detail, is the role accorded to Friday/Vendredi. For Defoe Friday's
sojourn on the island confirms the rectitude of Crusoe's conduct
and makes of his hero an ideal representative of Western, Calvinist culture. Vendredi's presence has the opposite effect. The
pagan black leads Robinson to a higher degree of self-knowledge

than he believes he could ever have found in Christian Europe.

It is a commonplace of literary scholarship to note that *Robinson Crusoe* is one of the first examples of the novel form in English.[4] What is less frequently appreciated is that *Robinson Crusoe* is among the last literary works to embody a totally coherent view of the relationship between man and God in the universe. At the basis of this novel is an absolute confidence that God really exists and that He provides Crusoe with signs that will become increasingly clearer as the shipwrecked seaman progresses along the road of Christian betterment.

For Robinson Crusoe, conduct that reflects the best interests of one's social class is a means to salvation, and social (economic) success is an indication of divine approval. As Crusoe tells his story, his first error was not to heed his father's (God's representative) advice and remain faithful to his appointed class, "the middle station." Instead, he squanders his money and, against his father's wishes, he goes to sea. Eventually, his unwise decision to enter the slave trade leads to shipwreck. The mistake here has nothing to do with the moral issue of slavery; Crusoe was greedy. His lust for money was pushing him beyond the bounds of the middle station.

The shipwreck is God's punishment, and the beginning of Crusoe's trials. He must not only rebuild his life, but almost literally re-create the economic development of England. Just like Tournier's Robinson, Crusoe starts out on the food-gathering, agrarian level and slowly progresses to a plateau of industrial development that approximates England's achievements at the time he was lost at sea. Throughout his struggles Crusoe is compelled by God to advance at the divine pace and not his own. For example, when Crusoe builds a canoe he takes it too far out to sea on the initial voyage and almost comes to grief. For him this is God's way of approving the progress he has made while at the same time warning him that he has not yet matured sufficiently to go beyond the limits of the island.

Friday's arrival is another sign from God. Not only does he now have a companion, but a slave as well. Friday will aid him in his economic and moral betterment. The first word that Crusoe teaches him is "Master," and in doing so he marks his development from a primitive, sinful state to a level of moral superiority that permits a hardworking, white Englishman to

employ a slave in order to improve his world and thus glorify
God.

Robinson Crusoe never thinks. He just interprets the transparent signs that God reveals to him. Yet in the context of Defoe's
novel, this attitude is perfectly justified. God indicates his will
in such a manner that a devout Christian need only understand
and obey.

When the rescue ship arrives, Crusoe is ready to leave. He
collects the money he has hoarded for twenty-eight years and
embarks for Europe. When he finally returns to England he
learns that he has inherited enough money to allow him to
live quite comfortably, the surest sign of divine approbation.

Tournier's view of *Robinson Crusoe*

Defoe's *Robinson Crusoe* is the sort of literature that Tournier
claims he does not like. It is an allegory, a work in which all
the meanings are fixed and ambiguity does not exist (at least
for Defoe) and where the entire story is a hymn to the Calvinist
work ethic. Of course, Tournier takes many events and details
from Defoe, but often it is for the sake of parody. For instance,
there is the famous moment in *Robinson Crusoe* where Crusoe's
tranquillity is shattered by the discovery of a cannibal's footprint.
Robinson makes a similar discovery and is suitably horrified
until he realizes that the footprint is his own. While Defoe's
novel might have been the starting point for Tournier, his real
interest and inspiration is the myth of Robinson Crusoe.

The New Robinson

The questioning of a society's values that one does not find
in *Robinson Crusoe* is present throughout *Vendredi, ou les limbes
du Pacifique*. At times this critique emerges from very precise
details. Defoe never gives the exact date when Crusoe's adventure begins, but Tournier does: 29 September 1759. Defoe
wrote his novel at the beginning of the eighteenth century,
between 1718 and 1723. This is before what is loosely termed
the Enlightenment had really begun. By setting the novel past
the century's mid-point and by having Robinson praise the
penny-pinching maxims of Ben Franklin (*Ve,* 116), Tournier

is able to question, much as Rousseau did, the intellectual complacencies of the Age of Reason.

Before Vendredi's arrival Robinson was certainly a troubled man, but a person nevertheless attempting to adhere to the virtues of rationality, hard work, and the superiority of urban to country life. (In a famous quarrel with Rousseau, Diderot said that to abandon the city for the countryside was to foresake the struggle for civilization.)[5] When Robinson accepts without demur both the destruction of his island civilization and the moral ascendency of Vendredi, he is adopting an iconoclastic, Rousseauian attitude toward progress and thus putting himself at odds with a major current of Western thought.

Crusoe named the savage Friday for no better reason than he happened to find him on a Friday. Robinson has a more complicated explanation: "Vendredi. This is neither the name of a person, nor a *nom commun,* it is midway between them, the name of a being half alive, half abstract, strongly marked by its temporal quality, fortuitous, and sort of episodic" (*Ve,* 123). Robinson is wondering, as did many of the Enlightenment philosophers, just where on the scale of humanity does this black creature find a place. In *Robinson Crusoe* the main character's racism is so intrinsic to his religious and social code that it fails to emerge as a significant element in the book. Crusoe is white, Friday is black; Crusoe is Christian and Friday pagan. Given these factors, Defoe and his contemporaries would have no difficulty justifying and indeed extolling Crusoe's treatment of the slave. Tournier, by the words he puts into Robinson's mouth, chooses to make the racist assumptions explicit in order to emphasize the "savagery" that suffuses this allegedly civilized period in human history.

Any twentieth-century reader of *Robinson Crusoe* is struck, even amazed, by Crusoe's indifference to his island's natural beauty. Condemned in his own mind to exile far from his peers, Crusoe never notices that his sun-filled island, blessed with mostly beautiful weather, fertile soil, abundant game, and devoid of dangerous animals, is as close to Paradise as most people could imagine. He yearns instead for dirty, wet, noisy Europe. Any notion of civilized man's alienation from nature is nonexistent in Defoe's novel, but it is a major concern for Tournier.

Before his world was turned upside down by the explosion,

Robinson's attitude toward Vendredi illustrated this alienation that modern man experiences before natural phenomenon. In *About Looking,* John Berger emphasizes the sentimentality that frequently characterizes urban dwellers' conduct toward animals and contrasts it with the realistic approach of country people.[6] Robinson has a profound, emotional attachment to Tenn, but he is surprised by the immediate affection that the dog shows toward Vendredi. Robinson realizes that the Vendredi who sleeps curled up beside Tenn would be quite capable of eating the animal if circumstances so dictated. He also suspects that the dog knows that, yet Tenn's closeness to Vendredi is more intense and visceral than any affection he has ever shown toward Robinson.

The ease that Vendredi has with his animals, plants (at one point Vendredi camouflages himself so successfully in a tree that he appears to become part of it), and even his own body troubles Robinson as much as it fascinates him. Robinson enclosed a flock of sheep to facilitate their eventual slaughter; Vendredi prefers to hunt any animal he kills. This is certainly not time efficient, but it is fairer, since it provides the animal with the possibility of escape and, in the goat Andaor's case, of conquest.

Before Speranza exploded, Robinson insisted that Vendredi clothe his nudity. Without really understanding the point of this command, Vendredi nonetheless obeyed—at least for as long as Robinson was around. Vendredi's ability to wear clothing, however unwillingly, becomes a form of superiority over the white man, since if the savage can stand to wear pants, Robinson could never, until after the explosion, go naked. Robinson was frightened by this creature whose continuous laughter and joy at life contrasted with the civilized man's perpetual melancholy and, shortly before Speranza erupted, he began to see himself in a most unaccustomed way: "I begin to put myself in his place and I feel pity for this child . . . subject to all the fantasies of a mad man. My situation is even worse, because I see myself through my only companion as a sort of monster, as if I were looking into a distorting mirror" (*Ve,* 128).

Defoe's Robinson Crusoe is a Calvinist. His religion is rigid, exclusive, and permits no questioning of the Divine Will. Crusoe's religious orientation affects every aspect of his life. Tournier's Robinson is also marked by his religion. He is a Quaker (*Ve*, 24), a member of a religious community justly celebrated for its gentleness, tolerance, and efforts to treat others with love. Robinson's religious background has provided him with a degree of openness that is totally absent in Defoe's Crusoe.

Love is a quality almost completely lacking in *Robinson Crusoe*. If the hero tries to love, fear, and serve his God, it is the latter two qualities that predominate. There is no mention of physical love in *Robinson Crusoe*. Whereas Defoe is discreet, Tournier is explicit. Robinson does make love, first to a log whose shape reminds him of a woman's body, and then to the earth. With Speranza he engenders flowers, mandrakes to be exact, which he considers to be his children. Before the arrival of Vendredi, it is these moments of intimacy with the earth where Robinson comes closest to being happy.

Tournier's *Vendredi*

The brief comparison of *Robinson Crusoe* and *Vendredi, ou les limbes du Pacifique* indicates that the differences far outweigh the similarities. In *Vendredi* Tournier is not rewriting and updating Defoe's novel, he is re-creating the myth of Robinson Crusoe for a twentieth-century consciousness. To do this Tournier develops his work in a direction that is diametrically opposed to Defoe's. *Robinson Crusoe* celebrates the triumph of European values while *Vendredi* becomes an extensive critique of the cultural and sexual underpinnings of Western society. In *Vendredi* Tournier is not interested in offering ways of improving Western society. The goals that he had set for himself were more extreme, and in *Le Vent Paraclet* he insists that his purpose was to show the destruction of one form of civilization and then the "creation of a new world" (*VP*, 223).

Tournier chose Robinson Crusoe to be one version of Adam (the other is Vendredi) in his new world for a number of reasons. Tournier believes that "Robinson is one of the constitutive elements in the soul of Western man" (*VP*, 215). Robinson embodies, perhaps more than any other character in Western literature, the experience of solitude, and for Tournier solitude is "the most pernicious wound of contemporary Western man" (*VP*, 215). Although Defoe's Crusoe complains of his solitude, his

confidence in an omnipresent deity belies this claim. In Tournier's version of the myth, Robinson, despite his prayers, fasting,
and biblical readings, is essentially alone.

Robinson's life on the island takes him through three stages
of development, but contrary to the levels of knowledge that
Spinoza describes in his *Ethics,* they are not necessarily hierar-
chical, nor are the latter two so radically dissimilar as they may
first appear. The three stages are the experience of despair in
"la souille," the efforts to Westernize and administer the island,
and then the progression toward "la cité solaire" ("the City
of the Sun") that follows Robinson's conversion to Vendredi's
world view. Although the second and third stages appear quite
different and seem to represent a positive development for Robinson, they both stem from the hero's dominant personal characteristic. As already noted, Captain Van Deyssel told Robinson
that he is an organizer who "struggles against a world in disorder and labors to control it by whatever means are at hand"
(*Ve,* 7).

Robinson's passage from stage two to stage three will constitute a radical change in the way he orders experience, but it
remains to be considered whether all these transformations conform to anything outside of Robinson's imagination. One cannot
forget that Robinson's tarot card is "le bateleur" ("mounte-
bank," "buffoon") whose creation "is illusion and whose order
is illusory" (*Ve,* 7). Robinson, like all of Tournier's heroes, is
obsessed by order, and thus may be prone to think he has discovered what he might in fact have created.

"La souille" dominates when the island is called Desolation.
It is the novel's image for unbridled nature, the world as chaos.
Robinson retreats to "la souille" when he loses all hope, when
he is unable to control either his mind or his body: "He ate,
his nose pressed against the earth, unnamable things. He defe-
cated and rarely avoided rolling about in the soft warmth of
his own excrement" (*Ve,* 34).

"La souille," with its tepid waters and signs of burgeoning
life, "the slime on which clouds of mosquitoes were dancing
was agitated by viscous eddies when a boar, whose speckled
groin alone emerged, grasped onto its mother's flank" (*Ve,* 33),
is also a womb, but one from which no human life is supposed
to come forth. What Robinson thinks of in "la souille" concerns

only his past which alone has "an existence and a significant value" (*Ve,* 34). The purpose of these reflections is to ease him into death: "Death was coming; it was the long-awaited moment when he could finally delight in this mine of accumulated gold (his thoughts of the past)" (*Ve,* 34–35).

At this juncture Robinson's state of mind resembles that of a *secondaire* to the extent that the past has become a burden that charms as it crushes. Unlike the *secondaire,* however, Robinson is not an artist. A hallucination causes him to see his deceased sister on a ship, and this vision drags him from "la souille." What keeps him from returning there is the one modest creative instinct he possesses: "He would once again take his destiny in hand. He would work" (*Ve,* 35).

Speranza is his first creation, the first fruit of his labor. When Robinson was shipwrecked he was terrified but not immediately prey to total despair. It was in this state that he first noticed something odd about the island: "It suddenly struck him that the island, its rocks and forests, was nothing other than the eyelid and eyebrow of an immense eye, blue and humid, gazing at the sky" (*Ve,* 21). This vaguely anthropomorphic image disquieted Robinson, but it also inspired him to undertake some means of escape. The result was the construction of the ill-fated *Evasion.* The failure to launch the boat provoked a despair that led him back to "la souille."

After the hallucinatory appearance of his sister, Robinson's resolve to start working again leads to the island's taking on a more pronounced form: "It seemed to him that, looking at the map of the island in a certain way . . . , it could be the profile of a woman's body without a head, a woman, yes, seated with her legs under her in an attitude that mingled submission, fear, and simple abandon" (*Ve,* 40). Desolation has become Speranza.

Robinson's attitude toward Speranza provides the best illustration of his need to create order, to force the exotic and terrifying into some comprehensible mold. Without any qualms or second thoughts, he begins to define his relationship to Speranza in terms of courtship: "I will triumph . . . only to the extent that I will know how to accept my island for what she is and in turn be accepted by her" (*Ve,* 44). Yet, like many a young man in love, Robinson's idea of accepting Speranza for what

she is involves changing her: "This massive dose of rationality
that I want to administer to Speranza, will I find the resources
for it within myself?" (*Ve*, 57–58). He will organize and con-
struct in an effort to woo Speranza, and it will only be after
many accomplishments—the building of his home, his enclosure
of the sheep, and the foundation of the Conservatory of Weights
and Measures—that he permits himself the pleasure of entering
the cave that leads to Speranza's womb.

It is tempting to dismiss this courtship as bizarre nonsense,
as an excellent indication that Van Deyssel was right when he
said that a person like Robinson never understands just how
illusory his order is. Yet whatever Robinson's powers of self-
delusion are, and they may prove to be considerable, his sexual
fantasies with Speranza play a significant role in the novel.

Sexuality

Beginning with *Vendredi* and continuing through *La Roi des
Aulnes* and *Les Météores* Tournier seems to explore a theory of
sexual expression that contrasts sharply with standard Freudian-
ism. Yet what makes an analysis of Tournier's position somewhat
difficult is that it emerges through characters who, like Robinson,
tend toward self-delusion. If this technique occasionally proves
frustrating to the critic, it has the great advantage of suggesting
new attitudes about sexual expression without appearing to re-
place one form of dogmatism (Freudian) with another. A reader
of Tournier must be aware that nowhere in his writings is he
opting for one form of sexual activity over another. What matters
for him is the enormous ambiguity and complexity of human
sexuality, a subject that due to religious and social pressures
has remained largely unexamined.

Sexuality appears in Tournier's novels under two aspects.
There is the general philosophic issue of its meaning and ramifications, but there is also its literary role: how sexuality is understood or misunderstood by characters for whom it is but one
factor in their complicated personalities. Throughout his novels
Tournier constantly manipulates these two sides of the question.
He intrigues, annoys, and, at least in *Les Météores,* enrages, but
he never preaches.

In *Vendredi* Robinson's development constitutes a challenge to Freud's notion of the polymorphous perverse. According to Freud children are naturally polymorphous perverse, which means that they find all parts of their bodies, as well as objects in general, sources of erotic delight.[7] The maturing process, with its concomitant socialization of the individual, leads a person to associate sexual satisfaction entirely with the genital area since, for Freud, the purpose of sexual activity is procreation.

When Robinson arrived on the island he was a mature man whose sexual life was perfectly normal. (Unlike Defoe's Crusoe, Tournier gives Robinson a wife and children whom he left in England.) What happens on the island, however, could be described as a return to the polymorphous perverse. The log, the cave, and the earth he fecundates are initially substitutes for a woman's body, but eventually at least the cave and the earth (he abandons the log when he is stung inopportunely by an insect inside it) become objects of erotic delight in themselves. Through them Robinson makes love to Nature.

Freud viewed the individual's sexual development as linear; there was a form of sexual interest and expression appropriate for every stage up until adulthood, but any regression to an earlier level was a sign of illness. Yet in Speranza's cave Robinson discovers that regression can be a form of growth.

Tournier began by linking Robinson's conquest of Speranza with the normal work and courtship ethic. The young man succeeds in business and thereby wins the lady. However, once Robinson possesses Speranza, the intensity of the experience leads to a reversal of ordinary values and reactions. What Robinson finds in the cave is not the pleasure of intercourse, but the peace of the womb. In Speranza's deepest recesses he must assume the fetal position. Here Robinson is calm, at one with himself and in the process of reliving the experience of an unborn child. Robinson has managed as an adult to reach backward in time and reestablish contact with his prenatal self.

Outside of Speranza is a world of clear distinctions, where everything has its unchanging place. Yet in the cave these distinctions dissolve. Robinson begins to suspect that he is Speranza (*Ve,* 82), that what he has conquered is not the female Speranza but his own maleness, so that now his hitherto latent feminine qualities can begin to emerge.

At the same time, Robinson begins to speculate about the

possible existence of another, hidden island (*Ve,* 80)—that Speranza is a woman, himself, and something else as well. Just what
this "something else" is he cannot determine by himself, but
must await the arrival of Vendredi.

Vendredi, the Character

When Vendredi tosses a lighted pipe into Speranza's cave,
the flame ignites the gunpowder Robinson had hidden there.
This powder is one of the last symbols of Robinson's fading
Western culture, and Speranza literally spews it from the earth.
The explosion kills Tenn, and Robinson now has no further
ties with his past. Europe, civilization, and the work ethic are
now behind him. Robinson is about to enter the City of the
Sun.

In a radio interview Tournier described Vendredi as "a sort
of Adam, representing virginity."[8] In *Le Vent Paraclet* he says
that "the principle of Vendredi is aerial, Aeolian, and Arielish"
(*VP,* 228). Vendredi would seem to be an uncorrupted and
pure force of nature. Yet in the novel he is largely a cipher.
Just as Robinson's speculations create an identity or a series
of identities for Speranza, he also, by dint of his continuous
interpretations of his young friend's acts, creates the person
who is Vendredi. What Robinson mostly finds in Vendredi are
qualities that are the opposite of his own. Vendredi is refractory
to economy, hard work, and organization, the bases of Robinson's initial conquest of the island. Vendredi is instinct and
Robinson understanding, but it is not until the novel's end that
Robinson perceives the less innocent side of Vendredi: how
easily he is tempted by the novelties aboard the British ship
and how readily he abandons the island that Robinson has considered his friend's natural home.

Just as Robinson discovered himself to be Speranza at a particular moment, he has a comparable revelation with Vendredi.
Not that he ever sees himself as another Vendredi; he would
like that, but knows it can never completely happen: "the man
of the earth, torn from his hole by the aeolian spirit, has not
himself become aeolian" (*Ve,* 182). Instead, Robinson decides
that Vendredi's victory over the ram, Andaor, is the savage's
conquest of himself since "Andaor, that's me" (*Ve,* 36). Andaor
is a creature of the earth, like the mythical Anteus, indomitable

as long as his feet touched the ground. Vendredi is the young Hercules who subdues his mighty foe by driving him off a cliff. This, however, is not the end of the adventure. By fashioning a kite from the ram's skin and turning his skull into an aeolian harp, Vendredi fulfills his promise to make Andaor fly and sing. Robinson, himself a creature of the earth, associates with the ram. He becomes, through Vendredi's intervention, free from the normal world where rationality dominates. Robinson continues his ascent to what he takes to be higher levels of consciousness. He learns to overcome his horror of nudity and the unexpected; for the first time in his life he is at ease with his body and his natural environment.

With Vendredi, as with Speranza, Robinson's sexual liberation continues. He notices that he never has any physical desire for his friend (*Ve,* 184), but this has nothing to do with traditional moral taboos. By the time Vendredi arrived on the island, "my sexuality had already become *elementary,* and it was toward Speranza that it turned" (*Ve,* 184). Inspired by Vendredi, Robinson finds himself moving beyond the usual forms of love, toward a union with nature in all its force. He associates this with the sun: "If it were necessary to translate into human terms this solar copulation, it would be in feminine terms, and it would be suitable to describe me as the wife of the sky" (*Ve,* 185). Robinson quickly adds that even this analogy is misleading. At the level at which he finds himself, "the difference between the sexes has been overcome" (*Ve,* 185) and he has given his masculinity and his femininity, his entire being to this island world that he loves.

Myth

Robinson's efforts to understand himself lead him more and more into the realm of myth, but this development is not without a degree of confusion: "Venus, the Swan, Leda, the Dioscuri . . . I grope about in search of myself amid a forest of allegories" (*Ve,* 187). Robinson's reference to the Dioscuri (all the other figures mentioned are associated with this central story), as well as the confusion that surrounds his understanding of himself in relation to this myth, heighten the ambiguity of the novel's end.

The Dioscuri (i.e., sons of Zeus) were twins whose mother

was Leda, daughter of Thestius, king of Aetolia. Their names were Castor and Pollux. The popular imagination (perhaps also Robinson's) associated these brothers primarily with the idea of inseparable friendship, but the story is more complex.[9] Zeus, in the guise of a swan, made love to Leda. She produced *two* sets of twins; Pollux and Helen were the offspring of the god, but Castor and Clytemnestra were the children of Leda's mortal husband, Tyndareus, who had slept with her on the same night as she was visited by Zeus. When the mortal brother, Castor, was killed in battle, Pollux intervened with Zeus in order to rescue him from the underworld. Zeus yielded to his son's pleas and eventually both brothers were deified and became the constellation Gemini, "the Twins."

In Tournier's terms these brothers are imperfect twins, but what is more important is that one of them, Pollux, by his divine origins, is clearly superior to the other. For Robinson Vendredi is the greater, since after the explosion he attempts to model himself on his savage brother. While this is Robinson's viewpoint, the myth he evokes would suggest otherwise. Vendredi succumbs at the end, not Robinson. By yielding to the temptations of the British crewmen, Vendredi is condemning himself to perpetual slavery, a more modern version of life in the underworld. Also, quite apart from Robinson's narration of events and his interpretations of their meanings, it is obvious from what happens in the novel that Vendredi is a person typical of his culture, just as was Robinson at the beginning. Much like Robinson, Vendredi neither loved nor hated the way he lived in his society. Indeed, the question was never even asked, since on Speranza he lived more or less as he had always lived. Circumstances forced Robinson to reexamine his values, but no such circumstances existed for Vendredi. When beguiled by things he does not understand (the ship and the activities of the crew), he leaves Robinson without a qualm and thus seals his doom. Just as Pollux had to intercede with Zeus in order to immortalize his brother, it had been Robinson's efforts throughout the third portion of the novel that created the greatness of Vendredi.

The originality of Tournier's use of myth in all his writings is that he allows for the possibility that his characters might not really understand the myths they evoke. This will have disastrous consequences in *Le Roi des Aulnes*. This is not the case in *Vendredi*, but Robinson's misunderstanding of the Dioscuri does cast doubts on some of the "revelations" he has toward the novel's end. After all, revelation and confusion can be difficult to separate in any context, and this novel's at times effusive prose can frustrate as often as it charms. This is perhaps what annoyed an American critic who wrote that *Vendredi* was "*Robinson Crusoe* rewritten by Freud, Walt Disney, and Claude Lévi-Strauss" (*V*, 387).

Throughout his years on the island Robinson has developed a critique of Western society that has its degree of coherence. He has confronted and triumphed over solitude and racism (Tournier had wanted to dedicate this novel to the much abused immigrant workers in France, but out of modesty decided against it [*VP*, 230]). Robinson has also struggled to widen his understanding of human sexuality. Yet this same man has always been something of a fool, a creator and victim of his own illusions. Robinson's passion for structure is so great that he is quite capable of confusing the discovery of an order that actually exists with the invention of a world that is nothing other than a reflection of his personal needs and fantasies.

Gilles Deleuze, a distinguished psychologist and longtime friend of Tournier, points to the essential element in the happiness Robinson finds at the novel's end: "Robinson's final goal is 'dehumanization,' the meeting of the libido with the free elements, the discovery of a cosmic energy or a great elementary health that can only come forth on the island."[10] What matters here is Deleuze's insistence that Robinson must remain on the island. The identity of the hidden island whose existence Robinson suspected is found in the literal translation of the novel's title, *Friday, or the limbo of the Pacific*. This hidden island is limbo, that special place invented by St. Augustine where the souls of unbaptized children dwell. Limbo is neither heaven nor hell; it is a world removed from either extreme and from ordinary human concerns as well. There is no escape from limbo, but there is no hardship there either. In his autobiographical and critical writings Tournier never discusses what he means by limbo, but he does speak of Robinson's island. He says that the island is "a closed garden" and "the geographical equivalent of the absolute" (*VP*, 291). The absolute is "etymologically

that which has no rapport, no relation" (*VP,* 290), apparently
a state where one is free of life's normal pressures. Tournier
also suggests that "if Robinson refuses to leave Speranza it is
because he senses the terrible aging that will attend his social
reintegration" (*VP,* 292). This absolute state, coupled with the
reference to limbo in the title, imply that Robinson has somehow
become a child again. Yet the novel denies this. At the end
of *Vendredi* Robinson has the thoughts, fears, and ultimately
the joys and responsibilities of an adult. However, his isolation
in a place that he totally controls creates for him a situation
akin to limbo. Here Robinson can live exactly as he wants:
he can educate the child according to his lights, he can pursue
his dialogue with the elements, and all the while rest assured
that his ideal existence will never be disturbed (Robinson had
asked the ship's captain to tell no one of his whereabouts). In
these circumstances the issue of whether Robinson is responding
to truth or illusion becomes irrelevant. To borrow a phrase
from the last page of *The Myth of Sisyphus,* we should believe
Robinson happy.

A Child's Version

Vendredi, ou les limbes du Pacifique has had several offshoots.
It was made into a film for television starring Michael York,
and in 1973 Antoine Vitez and Michel Raffaelli presented a
stage version at the Palais de Chaillot in Paris. While Tournier
did some consulting for these projects, he was not directly involved in refashioning his text according to the exigencies of
stage and screen. He has, however, written another version
of *Vendredi* for children. This is *Vendredi ou la vie sauvage* (Friday,
or the savage life).

Tournier has done other children's books (see the bibliography) and claims that he would like to do a child's version of
everything he writes,[11] but *La Vie Sauvage* is by far his most
famous and popular book for children. The plot follows that
of *Vendredi* with several additions and changes of detail. Tournier spends more time describing the island and the animals
that live there, at one point Robinson and Vendredi develop
a sign language to communicate; the sexual elements are muted
(Tournier has Vendredi sleeping with a young goat which he

says represents sexuality),[12] and the obsessive side of Robinson's personality is toned down (at one point Robinson mentions that he is making laws to govern the island in the event that others arrive).[13]

The most striking aspect of *La Vie Sauvage* is, except for the goat, the absence of ambiguity. This is partly due to Tournier's use of third-person narration. Apart from the chapter in which Robinson writes out the island's laws, the story is told entirely in the third person by an omniscient narrator. In *Vendredi,* Tournier switches back and forth between the first and third person. In *La Vie Sauvage,* the continuous third-person narration provides the young reader with a single, steady voice that not only describes events, but frequently explains their significance. For example, Tournier makes clear Robinson's hoarding food is a form of avarice (*VS, * 34), that Robinson associated leaving the island with death (*VS,* 138), and that Vendredi condemned himself to slavery by sailing off on the British ship (*VS,* 148).

What makes *La Vie Sauvage* interesting for literary criticism is the importance that Tournier ascribes to writing for youngsters. He obviously loves children, enjoys speaking with them in schools, and believes that they can respond well to good writing.

Tournier thinks that children's books are, or at least should be, literature. He says that writing for children presents the greatest of difficulties and that a book that a child cannot read is "less good."[14] In an interview with *Elle* magazine he suggested that "a child's book teaches us better and more profoundly about the society that produced it than any other literary expression."[15]

In speaking about *La Vie Sauvage* Tournier stressed the seriousness of his intentions. He believes that books for children should be eroticized, "perhaps even in a more intense manner than books for adults."[16] The sexuality of which he speaks is "a free sexuality of which children have a vague awareness."[17] In comparing *Vendredi* and *La Vie Sauvage* he wonders which is the version for children and which for adults, which is the original and which the copy.[18] At the same time, Tournier says that *La Vie Sauvage* is the soul of *Vendredi* and that all that he has written or will write is childlike.[19]

It is difficult to accept Tournier's somewhat contradictory

judgments about *La Vie Sauvage.* While it is certainly a nice story for children, adults miss the subtlety and ambiguity of *Vendredi.* Yet, even given Tournier's considerable talent for hyperbole, his comments do reflect a genuine distaste for the rigid demarcation between the worlds of children and adults. When Tournier writes for children he is allowing for the limits of their life experience, but he is employing the same approach to literature that he uses in his "adult" novels. He tells an interesting story and does not indulge in stylistic complexities. A child can readily handle a straightforward narrative and an educated adult has little difficulty with some shifting of voice. However, within this traditional format Tournier manages to engender thoughts, suggest possible modes of behavior and viewpoints about others that take the reader into areas that he has perhaps not previously explored.

Chapter Three
Le Roi des Aulnes

Nazi Kitsch

In March 1982 Saul Friedländer, a distinguished historian who had studied anti-Semitism and nazism, published a book called *Reflets du Nazisme* (Reflections of Nazism). Friedländer was interested in the recent spate of films and novels about the Nazi phenomenon. The films included Werner Fassbinder's *Lili Marleen*, Hans Jürgen Syberg's *Hitler, a Film about Germany*, and Louis Malle's *Lecombe Lucien*. Among the novels were George Steiner's *The Portage to San Cristóbal of A. H.* and Michel Tournier's *Le Roi des Aulnes*. Friedländer allows that these works can illuminate interesting angles of the Nazi experience, but he finds them somewhat disturbing because of the fascination they display for twisted sexuality, death, power imagery, and the personality of Adolph Hitler. He notes that many of these works appeared at the same time as the pornographic industry began to exploit Nazism for reasons that had little to do with art.[1] While Friedländer appreciates the difference between pornography and the work of serious artists, he also recognizes that the flirtation with so many questionable themes leaves the viewer of *The Night Porter* or the reader of *Le Roi des Aulnes* with a certain uneasiness.[2] Friedländer is particularly disturbed by the fact that the main character in Tournier's novel becomes a toy of occult powers which appear to remove from him any responsibility for his acts.[3]

Friedländer insists that he has no expertise in film or literary criticism and that he is nothing other than a "naive" spectator or reader.[4] Yet this modest avowal enhances Friedländer's credibility. He is the honest, intelligent person who, when he reads Abel Tiffauges's frequently muddled meditations on the cosmic significance of his deeds, cannot forget that this "hero" is indirectly responsible for the deaths of hundreds of adolescents.

The Story

The story line of *Le Roi des Aulnes* would appear to justify Friedländer's uneasiness. Abel Tiffauges is a gigantic, myopic car mechanic who has considerable difficulty coping with daily life in pre–World War II France. As a small, frail child he was placed by unloving parents in a home called St. Christopher's. Here a strapping boy named Nestor befriended him. After a stupid prank in a church backfires Abel runs away, but he is sent back by his father. Upon his return to St. Christopher's the boy learns that Nestor has been killed in an accident. The jolt of his friend's death provokes the beginnings of a physical transformation in Abel. He starts to grow quickly; he becomes big and strong, but suffers from failing eyesight. By the end of his adolescence he has become the image of Nestor.

Abel likes women, but he prefers children more. He especially enjoys what he calls *"la phorie,"* which is the act of carrying a child on one's shoulders. He also becomes interested in photographing children and starts to follow one little girl in particular. One day she is molested in a tunnel and she incorrectly names Abel as her attacker. However, the outbreak of World War II saves Abel from prison; he is assigned to the communications branch of the army where he develops an expertise in dealing with carrier pigeons. Abel Tiffauges is captured by the Germans during the first day of actual fighting in World War II.

Abel's internment in a prisoner of war camp in northern Germany proves to be his liberation. He loves Germany, this country of "black and white" (*R,* 18) that appears so devoid of the complications of daily living that haunted him in France. Everything is strictly regulated in the camp. Abel works on an irrigation project, but this manual labor leaves his mind free to contemplate his personal destiny. He even manages to find a little cabin, hidden in the neighboring forest, and this place, which he calls "Canada," becomes his secret retreat.

Abel's hard work and docility earn him the trust of the German authorities and he receives a series of promotions. For a time he works as a forester at Rominten, the hunting retreat of Göring, and he gets to observe the great man close at hand. His final assignment is to Kaltenborn, a gigantic fortress in northern Prussia. As part of the Nazi war effort, Kaltenborn has been converted into a *napola,* which is a school that trains boys for eventual service in the S.S.

Abel considers all the changes in his life to be part of some profound pattern that he is struggling to decipher. For Abel Tiffauges, nothing can happen by chance. "Everything is a sign" (*R,* 13), and all the signs pertain directly to him. One day Abel discovers that he can write with his left hand as well as his right. This constitutes immediate proof that: "I am . . . provided with two types of writing. One is *adroite,* amiable, social, commercial; it reflects the masked person I pretend to be in society's eyes. The other is *sinistre,* deformed by all the clumsiness of genius, filled with lightening bolts and cries, inhabited in a word by Nestor's spirit" (*R,* 39). What would have been for a less enthusiastic interpreter the simple indication that a personality has its public and private side, becomes for Abel a revelation with vast and somber implications.

One day some German workers dig up the embalmed body of a man who died centuries ago. Shortly thereafter they find the equally ancient remains of what could be a child. The German doctor who examines the adult corpse dubs it "der Erlkö-nig" ("le roi des aulnes"). Abel is much impressed by these findings and associates himself with "der Erlkönig." Later, at Kaltenborn, he follows with horrified fascination some of the disgusting experiments of a Nazi scientist. He also meets an elderly German count who explains to him the complex laws that govern heraldic symbols, and Abel comes to believe that this arcane knowledge will eventually help clarify his destiny.

As the war begins to go badly for the Germans more and more S.S. adults are taken from Kaltenborn to serve at the front. This results in Abel assuming an increasingly important role. He becomes the person who rides about Prussia on a horse named Blue Beard and recruits children for the *napola.* Eventually he even takes charge of the boys' health and leads them through elaborate, quasi-religious ceremonies.

On one of his recruiting trips Abel stumbles upon the half-dead body of a Jewish boy, Ephraim. Abel attempts to nurse the boy back to health, but in doing so he begins to discover how badly he had misinterpreted the various symbols he associated with his destiny. He learns among other things that his Canada has a terrifying parallel. Ephraim explains that "Canada"

was the name given at Auschwitz to the room where the Nazis
would store the valuables they stole from the gassed Jews.

The destruction of Abel's symbolic universe parallels the collapse of the Nazi war effort. The Russian army arrives at Kaltenborn and Abel's young charges put up an insane and futile
resistance. As the fortress goes up in flames and the boys are
slaughtered, Abel tries to escape with Ephraim on his shoulders.
He manages to get out of Kaltenborn but only to sink into
the mud of a swamp. The last thing he sees before disappearing
into the slime is a six pointed star that shines in the heavens.

The Novel in Everyday Life

The story line of *Le Roi des Aulnes* appears to confirm a number
of Friedländer's fears. The novel seems to be replete with sado-
masochistic allusions, child molestation, and "perverse" sexual
interests on the part of the hero. The Nazi background only
heightens the intensity of all these elements. It is impossible
to deny that on the literal level *Le Roi des Aulnes* is a disturbing
book. Nonetheless, a more careful reading indicates that the
novel's purpose is not to detail the varieties of pornographic
experience.

Michel Tournier's *Le Roi des Aulnes* is a novel about literature;
both the literature consciously conceived by an artist and the
bastardized form of fictionalizing that transpires in Abel Tiffauges's head. This novel constitutes Tournier's most extensive
treatment of one of his major themes: the role of fiction and
fictionalizing in the daily lives of ordinary human beings.

Everyone knows that a novel, no matter how autobiographical,
contains elements that are invented. The author consciously creates scenes, characters, and events that might never have happened but which contribute to the story he wishes to tell. This
common understanding of what a novelist does can lead to the
facile distinction between the "make-believe" of literature and
what actually happens in "real life." The weakness in such a
distinction is that it allows one to overlook the important role
that "make-believe," that is, fictionalizing, plays in the ordinary
individual's life. For most people daydreams, fantasies about
the past and future are a constant, albeit somewhat unconscious,
occurrence. It is at once true and irrelevent that most people's

fantasies would probably constitute bad art; what matters is that the fictionalizing process is not confined to literature.

It is possible to read the final pages of *Vendredi* as an example of a man (Robinson) yielding totally to the fictive world he has created for himself. Yet however one chooses to read the ending of *Vendredi,* Robinson does harm to nobody. His island paradise/prison protects him from others and others from him. Things are different in *Le Roi des Aulnes.* Abel Tiffauges's conflation of truth and fiction leads to death and destruction. If *Vendredi* celebrated the beneficient power of fiction in daily life, *Le Roi des Aulnes* explores the destructive capacity of those who confuse what they want to be with the ways things are.

Goethe in the Third Reich

Abel shares with his Nazi captors an ability to distort reality to suit his own purposes. The parallel between Abel and the Nazis is one of the most important aspects of the novel and Tournier develops it in several ways. One of the most compelling ways is through an elaborate series of allusions to the artistic and scientific works of Goethe.

The phrase "le roi des aulnes" is the French translation of the German expression "der Erlkönig." Tournier's fascination with Goethe's poem begins with the strange story of its inception. This is how Tournier tells it in *Le Vent Paraclet:*

At the origin of this poem is an error in translation made by Herder who popularized Danish folklore in Germany. He turned "Eller," the elves, into "Erlen," the alder trees, because in the dialect spoken in Mohrungen (East Prussia), Herder's hometown, "alder" was pronounced "Eller." Now it is not very likely that Goethe was interested by the legend of the banal elf king. On the other hand, his imagination was excited by the precise and original evocation of the alder, because the alder is the black and harmful tree of dead waters. (*VP,* 115)

German scholars have tended to discuss the poem, "der Erlkönig," in relation to Goethe's life and psyche. The late K. R. Eissler, in his monumental *Goethe: A Psychoanalytical Study, 1775–1786,* suggests that the poem indicates some latent homosexual tendencies in the young poet.[5] The line in the poem used to justify this sort of interpretation, and the very line Tournier isolates is: "Ich liebe dich. Mich reizt deine schöne Gestalt" ("I love you. Your beautiful form excites me"). Tournier notes that the traditional French rendering, "Je t'aime. Ton doux visage me charme" ("I love you. Your sweet face charms me"), removes the verse's sexual innuendos. For reasons that will shortly be clear, he himself prefers "Je t'aime. Ton beau corps me tente" ("I love you. Your beautiful body tempts me" [*VP,* 116–17]). For Tournier, the frightened boy is a temptation, but the precise nature of the temptation is not made explicit.

In *Le Roi des Aulnes* Abel Tiffauges is tempted by little boys. Yet what he wants is not sexual gratification in the normal sense of the term. He wants, instead, *"la phorie,"* which, it will be recalled, is the experience of emotional satisfaction that comes from his carrying a child on his shoulders. *"La phorie"* is as innocent as it is bizarre. Nowhere in the novel does Abel molest a child, but he does seek and obtain a type of fulfillment that falls outside the established categories of homosexual and heterosexual love.

Abel's problem is not with his desire as such. What troubles him is that he cannot really accept that he is different from most people, and he struggles to offset his sense of inferiority by constantly proclaiming his superiority. He creates and then proceeds to inhabit a pseudomythical universe replete with signs, visions, and symbols whose true function is to justify an instinct, which is, of itself, neither good nor bad. Herein lies the basis for Tournier's references to "der Erlkönig" and his other uses of Goethe throughout the novel: Abel does on a microcosmic level what the Nazis accomplish on the macrocosmic scale. He twists and confuses his personal history in a way that resembles the Nazi perversion of their great German heritage. In *Le Roi des Aulnes,* Goethe is the symbol of Germany's distinguished past. Abel in the personal realm, and the Nazis in the area of culture and science, manage to distort something unique and make it appear disgusting.

The clearest example of Abel and the Nazis' mutual inability to view things honestly occurs when the German workers uncover the embalmed body of an ancient man. Practically nothing is known about the corpse, but this presents no serious obstacle to the Nazi pathologist charged with the autopsy. The doctor,

Professor Kiel, discreetly avoids commenting upon the corpse's most intriguing detail, a six-pointed star sewn on his cap, and immediately launches into an elaborate discourse that suggests, among other things, that the body might have taken its last meal at the precise moment of the Last Supper: "Thus at the very moment that the Judeo-Mediterranean religion was taking off in the Near East, an analogous rite was founded here, perhaps a parallel religion, strictly Nordic and even Germanic" (*R*, 201).

Abel is fascinated by such nonsense and is especially impressed when Kiel decides to name the corpse "le roi des aulnes," after Goethe's poem which, according to Kiel, is "the quintessence of the German soul" (*R*, 201). Should a reader choose to remember the more reliable Professor Eissler's opinion of the poem's significance, the good Nazi Kiel is certainly offering a startling assessment of the German character. In any case, what Abel and the Nazis share is an ability to turn fantasy into fact with lightning speed.

In the pages of *Le Vent Paraclet* Tournier often evokes the tragedy of Germany during the *Hitlerzeit:* "Germany, this machine able to make geniuses, has been broken by the man with the forelock and the little moustache" (*VP*, 143). Two Nazi researchers, Dr. Otto Blättchen and Dr. Otto Essig, appear in *Le Roi des Aulnes* and exemplify the misuse of Germany's scientific genius. What makes what they do particularly troubling is that their experiments are a parody of Goethe's scientific interests and accomplishments.

"This Mephisto in a white smock incarnated with a rare purity the S.S. laboratory type" (*R*, 264). With these words Tournier introduces Dr. Otto Blättchen, an "expert" on Aryan racial superiority whose experiments with the skulls of captured Jews and Russians demonstrate that the Israelites and the Bolsheviks are indeed the source of all "existing evil" (*R*, 264).

Blättchen's labors have some parallels with Goethe's own research. An important influence upon Goethe the scientist was a Dr. Gall, who is known today for his experiments in phrenology.[6] Goethe's interest in Gall's work led him to undertake his own examination of skulls and eventually he discovered the intermaxillary bone in human beings. The implications of Goethe's observations in this area go beyond the particular discovery, as significant as it was. The poet-scientist wrote a treatise

on the subject that was to become a milestone in the history
of comparative anatomy.[7] In addition, whereas Nazi experiments, such as Blättchen's, sought to establish the existence of
a master race that was unconnected to the lower species,
Goethe's work had just the opposite aim. As Rudolf Magnus
observed: "That Goethe's work was free of pre-conceived notions is most clearly shown by the manner in which he took it
for granted that man, from the aspect of comparative anatomy,
must be counted among the mammals."[8]

In contrast to the activities of Blättchen, the work of Dr.
Otto Essig is more ridiculous than nefarious. Essig's dissertation
subject, "La Méchanique symbolique à travers l'histoire de l'an-
cienne et de la nouvelle Germanie" (The symbolic mechanics
throughout the history of ancient and new Germania), apparently provides him with the expertise needed to discourse at
length and in the presence of Göring about a new means of
classifying deer antlers.

Dr. Essig's fanciful efforts at categorizing deer antlers constitutes a parody of Goethe's experiments in comparative anatomy
and plant classification. Goethe sought to ascertain how each
individual animal and plant was "so perfectly and harmoniously
developed."[9] His speculations eventually led him to a theory
of the correlation of parts, which, according to Magnus, "has
proven extraordinarily fruitful in the growth of science."[10] Essig
propounds a confusing theory about the relation between various sorts of antlers and the personalities of the creatures who
sport them, but his real contribution is to demonstrate, in a
novel where theorizing abounds, that however valuable an idea,
it is never without its potentially absurd applications: "And in-
clining toward Göring, he sketched a parallel between an antler
and the baton of a marshall that would not be much of a weapon
in combat, but which would render him physically untouchable
by the dignity it conferred" (R, 230).

Tournier's portraits of the Nazi scientist as Mephisto and as
sycophant illustrate, by their allusions to Goethe, the extent
to which a distinguished tradition of learning and discovery
had been made to serve criminal interests. At the same time,
the Nazi "search for truth" provides an all too obvious parallel
with Abel's cogitations.

Goethe's most famous work is certainly *Faust*. In a novel

that makes so much of Goethe, it is not surprising that *Faust* should play a prominent role. In *Le Roi des Aulnes* Tournier indulges the ambiguity of "der Erlkönig" and parodies Goethe's scientific achievements. When it comes to *Faust,* Tournier takes another tack: he reverses the progress of Goethe's tragedy until what had marked stages of development for Faust are signs of degeneracy for Abel Tiffauges.

Faust only becomes important in the novel once Abel enters Germany, "this country of black and white." Yet the event that precipitates Abel's conscription into the French army provides an ironic foretaste of what is to come. Abel was accused of molesting a little girl, a charge that was unfounded. In a sense, however, this incident constitutes Gretchen's revenge. In *Faust* the hero does seduce an innocent young girl, Gretchen, who, in a fit of depression, murders their illegitimate child. Gretchen is executed as a result, but Faust continues on to greater things. The last meeting of Gretchen and Faust comprises the final scene of *Faust, Part I.* Abel's encounter with the little girl takes place toward the end of the first section of *Le Roi des Aulnes,* but here Tournier reverses the scene. The girl escapes relatively unscathed and Abel goes to prison and then into battle.

Abel's first assignment as a prisoner of war in Germany is to participate in a massive irrigation project. This obvious reference to *Faust, Part II* serves a purpose that is the opposite of Goethe's. Goethe's Faust is transformed by his irrigation task and begins to develop a higher level of self-consciousness and humanity. Abel Tiffauges has no such luck. His enthusiasm for his work and his general fascination with Nazi Germany will only lead him progressively deeper into the moral and intellectual morass of the Third Reich.

The German word "tief" ("deep") is one of the most frequently employed words in *Faust.* [11] It suggests the goal of Faust's striving, especially in part 2, away from the ephemeral and toward the eternally valuable. "Tief" also figures prominently in Abel's surname, "Tiffauges." There is a moment in *Le Roi des Aulnes* where Dr. Blättchen offers a little disquisition on the Aryan implications of Abel's name:

He persuaded himself that Tiffauges was an alteration of *Tiefauge,* and consequently hid a distant Teutonic origin that made it all the more venerable. Henceforth he only calls me Herr Tiefauge, or, in his euphoric moments, he ennobles me, and I become Herr *von* Tiefauge.

That proves, he says to me, the purity of your blood, you are still the bearer to the highest degree of the particular sign that made the name valuable to your ancestoral namesake: *Tiefauge:* the deep eye, the eye plunged in the socket. And when people see you, Herr von Tiefauge, they understand so well this name that they wonder whether it isn't a nickname! (*R,* 277)

The truth, of course, is just the opposite. Abel Tiffauges is nearly blind, figuratively as well as literally. He has trouble seeing what is right before his eyes. At one point he collects hair shorn from the children in the *napola* during an S.S. induction ceremony and then asks a seamstress to make him a coat out of these tufts. The hideous parallel with the Nazi activities in the death camps is not lost on the seamstress, but Abel never sees the point.

After Blättchen's lecture, Abel briefly suspects that something is amiss. He knows that in German *tiefauge* is not far removed from *triefauge,* "sick, teary, watery eye" (*R,* 277). On a metaphorical level, this is a much better description of the quality of Abel's vision. Nonetheless, Abel's insight here, as on other occasions when he touches upon the truth, is temporary. Despite abundant evidence to the contrary, he persists in believing that some inner eye is leading him toward an overwhelming revelation.

This revelation he does have, but it is the opposite of what he expected and once again it involves a parody/reversal of *Faust.* Near the end of part 2, Faust is blinded, but the transformed hero does experience a great insight. In lines that begin "Die Nacht scheint *tiefer-tief* hereinzudringen" ("The night appeared deeper and deeper to inward draw"), Faust describes the beneficent effect God's Word has had on him.[12] As Faust utters these words angels are bearing him up to heaven.

It is toward the end of *Le Roi des Aulnes* that Abel discovers Ephraim, the Jewish child who reveals to him the horrors of Auschwitz. Abel is overwhelmed with disgust, but manages through desperate effort to get the boy and himself out of the *napola.* With Ephraim, who alternately proclaims him "the behemoth" and "the horse of Israel," on his shoulders, this latter-day *Erlkönig* staggers out of the fortress. Yet whereas Faust rose up to heaven, Abel Tiffauges can only sink into the mud.

Gilles de Rais

While the Goethe parallel is the most extensively elaborated one in the novel, there are others as well. They all emphasize the dichotomy between Abel's fictionalized self-image and the unpleasant truth. One of the most interesting parallels involves Abel's tendency to associate himself with literary, historical, or religious figures renown for their virtue or intelligence. For example, he views *"la phorie"* as part of a tradition that includes St. Christopher (the name of his boarding school), and the name of his friend Nestor, whose identity Abel claims to have assumed, calls to mind the Greek wise man of *The Iliad.* But there is one literary/historical figure who strongly resembles Abel and whom, predictably enough, Abel does not see. That is Gilles de Rais.

Gilles de Rais served with Joan of Arc in the wars against the English. A large, physically strong man, he was celebrated for his piety, generosity, and valor. By the age of twenty-eight he was already a "maréchal" ("field marshall") of France. It was only years later, as a result of a tax investigation, that the authorities discovered that throughout his adult life Gilles de Rais had been raping, torturing, and murdering children, perhaps as many as three thousand of them. Gilles was tried and executed at Nantes in 1440.

The chateau of Tiffauges was Gilles de Rais' favorite lodging, the place where he "got interested in magic," and where he "committed his most numerous crimes."[13] Scholars have frequently identified Blue Beard, best known from the short story by Perrault, with Gilles de Rais.[14] "Barbe bleue" (Blue Beard) is the horse Abel Tiffauges rides as he travels around northern Germany in search of children for the *napola.*

In his *Gilles de Rais,* Michel Bataille observes that "in peacetime Gilles would never have been able to discover, would never have had the chance to realize, that he had a taste for flowing blood. The war revealed it to him."[15] This exactly parallels Abel's situation. Without the war he might have remained a confused but harmless fellow whose fantasies rarely or never went beyond the limits of his mind. It is the freedom he finds in wartime Germany that permits his benighted efforts at self-discovery.

Shortly before his arrest and execution, Gilles de Rais was named a canon of a cathedral and began to dress like a cleric.[16] Tournier parodies this event when he has Abel, toward the novel's end, behave like a bishop at confirmation. He distributes a salve to his young charges in order to supplement their vitamin-deficient diet: "After dinner, the refectory becomes the theater of a strange and moving liturgy. The children come in a procession toward me, and I anoint them. . . . I raise my left hand, the index and middle finger joined, in a royal gesture of blessing" (R, 348).

As the Third Reich teeters on the verge of collapse, Abel intensifies his efforts to enlist boys for the school at Kaltenborn. At the same time, the Nazis accelerate their destruction of Jews, Gypsies, and other real or imagined opponents of Hitler. Both activities have a hideous precedent in Gilles's final days of freedom: "right up to the end, everything will be organized in such a way that the crescendo will be respected and an apparatus that will be more and more terrifying will unfold."[17] Throughout all this Gilles was urging his minions to "fire the ovens to their extreme."[18]

A final element in the analogy between Abel and Gilles concerns Gilles's execution. Once Gilles was condemned by the tribunal at Nantes, the actual carrying out of the sentence was turned, at the victim's own request, into something of a popular, religious festival. Gilles led a procession through the city's streets. The culminating act was his hanging. Tournier creates a contemporary version of this incident when he describes the French public's fascination with the guillotining of the mass murderer Franz Weidmann. Abel is present at this macabre ceremony, accompanied by a gossipy neighbor who exclaims when she sees Weidmann: "But, Mr. Tiffauges, doesn't he look like you . . . a person could say he was your brother" (R, 129).

Abel and Instincts

Abel's inability to understand the implications of an idea or event, and at times even to perceive the obvious, extends into the realm of instincts as well. Abel's personal delight in defecation, something he shared with his dead friend Nestor, leads him to champion the anal over the phallic instincts. The Horse, Abel's means of transportation at Kaltenborg, is "l'Ange Anal" (*R,* 241). The Deer, the prey of Nazi hunters and as such a transparent image of the children whom the S.S. conscript, is "l'Ange Phallophore" (*R,* 241). As so often occurs when Abel perceives a possible relationship, he contents himself with an interpretation that places the facts in some grandiose context while avoiding their concrete implications: "And Tiffauges was astonished to discover once again in progress the amazing inversion which in this murderous game (the hunt) turned the buttocksy, skittish beast (the horse) into a principle of aggression and extermination, and the king of the forest, whose antlers manifest his virility, into an unwilling prey, pleading for mercy" (*R,* 241).

In *L'Anti-Oedipe, Capitalisme et schizophrénie* (The anti-Oedipus, capitalism, and schizophrenia), Gilles Deleuze and Felix Guattari offer a commentary on anality that is germane to the treatment of the same subject in *Le Roi des Aulnes.* According to these authors: "It is the anal personality that tends toward sublimation; sublimation is completely anal."[19] *L'Anti-Oedipe* associates the anal personality and the proclivity for sublimation with the figure of the nomadic hunter, one of Abel's self-images. Deleuze and Guattari cite Pierre Clastres's description of "the solitary hunter who becomes one with his force and his destiny, and who sings in an increasingly rapid and distorted language, 'Me, Me, Me, I am a powerful nature, an irritated and aggressive nature.'"[20] In their concluding pages on anality and the nomadic hunter Deleuze and Guattari offer the wry suggestion that "No one ever died of contradiction," and then with regard to the results of ever-increasing contradictions: "From one pole to another, all the failures, all the defeats take place in a system that does not fail to be reborn from its own discordances."[21]

L'Anti-Oedipe provides the basis for a psychological portrait of Abel Tiffauges that is as unflattering as it is accurate, but which stands as an important counterweight to Abel's picture of himself. Sublimation is Abel's principal characteristic. No event can exist alone; everything must be forced into some vast pattern of signs and meanings whose relationship to Abel's real life is at best oblique. For Abel, every defeat or humiliation,

every embarrassing discovery of personal error, remains on one
level a new victory. He coins the term "inversion maligne"
("mischievous" or "malicious inversion") to justify his mis-
takes. The *"inversion maligne"* occurs when a sign actually indicates the opposite of what it appears to suggest. At one point
he speaks of children carrying toys as a sort of foreshadowing
of *"la phorie,"* a act normally done by adults. But then he notices
the boys in the *napola* playing with weapons and especially de-
lighting in riding on tanks, that is, the toy carrying the child.
This apparent contradiction is, however, quickly resolved: "I
come upon here, for the first time, a phenomenon of capital
importance, which is *the overturning of the 'phorie' by the 'inversion
maligne.'* It is, after all, logical that these two figures of my
symbolic mechanism come sooner or later to interfere with each
other" (*R,* 197).

Nazi Signs

The Nazis are equally gifted at sublimation and quick to create
their own variation of the *"inversion maligne."* When the old
count who lives at Kaltenborn learns of Abel's curious interest
in signs and symbols he offers to explain to him the code of
heraldry. In doing so the count indicates that the Nazis have
not only misused heraldic symbols, but have also sought to justify
their errors through labored interpretations:

It is always the case that the Prussian eagle has its head turned *à
dextra* as it should in the healthy heraldic tradition. Well, look at
the eagle of the Third Reich . . . its head is turned *à sinistra.* It's
an eagle twisted around, a true aberration, reserved for illegitimate
or decayed branches of noble families. Of course, no Party official
can justify this monstrosity. People discreetly alluded to it as a simple
blunder of the propaganda minister. Today Goebbels has finally found
an explanation: the eagle of the Third Reich looks toward the East,
toward the U.S.S.R. that it menaces and attacks. (*R,* 322)

Abel and the Nazis have much in common. By means of
various structuring devices (intellectual, mythic, racial) both
have forced the world into their narrow vision of it. Abel's
fictionalizing becomes increasingly dangerous and self-deluding

over the course of the novel, and as such his personal degrada-
tion accompanies the slow collapse of the Reich. His own death
and the destruction of the *napola* take place at the moment of
Germany's *Götterdämmerung*. The count ended his discussion
of Nazi heraldry reflectively: "The truth of the matter is that,
from its beginnings, the Third Reich was the product of symbols
which led the Nazis around" (*R,* 322). One aspect of the numerous distortions which permeated the Nazi ideology was that
their own symbols escaped their control. Reality was increasingly
shunted aside as the Party leaders searched for symbolic coherence at any cost. The count's judgment might be applied to
Abel as well.

Given the strong parallels between the Nazi mentality and
Abel's own, it is tempting to dismiss the hero of *Le Roi des
Aulnes* as a crypto-Nazi. Such a conclusion satisfies in the immediate, but is ultimately misleading. What appeals to Abel in Nazi
Germany is not the content of the ideology, but the effort to
create a perfectly ordered symbolic universe that excludes all
that is unsettling in life. Abel Tiffauges is haunted by *"la phorie"*;
he is drawn toward it, but cannot face this form of sexual difference as an individual. He therefore constructs a world that provides elaborate antecedents for himself and constant
encouragement from the "signs" he finds around him. Unlike
the Nazis, however, his aim is neither to destroy life nor to
propose himself as a model for others.

What Abel and the Nazis have in common is extremely troubling, but they are also significantly different. Abel wants to
express love in a form that disturbs him, while the Nazis reflect
their insecurities through a hatred for anyone judged dissimilar
to themselves. The former wants to express difference and the
latter to destroy it.

Michel Tournier has insisted that the veritable subject of *Le
Roi des Aulnes* is *"la phorie"* (*VP,* 120). If this is indeed the
case, what then is the significance of this seemingly bizarre notion and why is it linked to the Nazi experience? Whether or
not *"la phorie"* does represent some latent sexual need is a
subject for psychology rather than literary criticism. Nevertheless, it does have a literary value that is illuminated by its associa-
tion with World War II. As Hannah Arendt has shown in *The
Origins of Totalitarianism* and *Eichmann in Jerusalem,* World War

II shattered conventional notions about the goodness and self-
control inherent in human nature. The war revealed things about
ostensibly normal people's capacity for evil that have shocked
the world. Human nature has become at once more mysterious
and disturbing than ever before.

World War II has also forced a reexamination of the traditional ways of categorizing human instincts, among them the
sexual one. *"La phorie"* is one such attempt and Tournier linked
it to the war experience because, if there is any small positive
result from the destruction of World War II, it has to do with
a new willingness to question generally accepted beliefs about
human nature. If participation in the war provided Abel at least
with the potential for self-discovery, the knowledge gleaned
from the war makes the contemporary reader more aware of
the complexity, for good or for ill, of the human being.

Le Roi des Aulnes extends the discussion of human sexuality
that was begun in *Vendredi*. On the flyleaf of the Gallimard
edition of the novel, the writer, most probably Tournier, describes the book as "an essay to describe a new model of nongenital sexuality." *"La phorie"* is an example of nongenital
sexuality, but it would be wrong to limit *"la phorie"* to its literal
meaning. *"La phorie"* might well stand for any form of sexual
expression that seeks emotional gratification but does not aim
at reproduction.

Le Roi des Aulnes has many fine qualities. It tells a compelling,
troubling story; it makes a statement about the sorts of mentali-
ties that might have surfaced as a consequence of World War
II and even suggests a reevaluation of the sources of sexual
pleasure. Yet perhaps the novel's greatest merit lies in its demon-
stration of the interconnection of fact and fiction, life and literature.

The error that Saul Friedländer made in reading *Le Roi des
Aulnes* was to associate Abel Tiffauges's perspective with that
of his creator. Tournier portrays Abel as a deeply confused
individual who turns to elaborate but ultimately simplistic explanations of his own complexity. What makes it impossible to
categorize *Le Roi des Aulnes* as some contemporary version of
Nazi kitsch is not the "edifying" ending, which is really nothing
more than the final example of Abel's inability to achieve his

goals. Rather, it is the detailed description, throughout the novel, of how the intermingling of the real and the make-believe can become, with the right set of circumstances, the source of personal and even national havoc.

Chapter Four
Les Météores

Sanitary Problems

Les Météores (*Gemini*) created an uproar when first published. However, the controversy that surrounded the novel had none of the seriousness that pervades Friedländer's discussion of *Le Roi des Aulnes*. The problem was really one of hygiene. Robert Kanters fumed in the staid *Figaro littéraire* that in *Les Météores* there is a page concerning the relationship "between constipation and sexuality that I could not quote unless this newspaper were printed on toilet paper."[1] Kanters went on to add that the novel lacked "a sense of the spiritual life,"[2] a comment that is not surprising after the earlier remark. An English critic was comparably exercised by the book: "*Gemini . . .* should be flung on one of those rubbish dumps to which the author is so attracted."[3]

The character who provoked such critical outrage is Alexandre Surin, a cynical homosexual who combines a visceral hatred of the heterosexual world with a fascination for bowel movements and garbage dumps. His conduct is so extravagant and his comments so bizarre that he is for many reasons, and for better or worse, the novel's main attraction. Several critics have noted that when Alexandre dies, about two thirds of the way through the book, *Les Météores* loses much of its interest.

Tournier insists that Alexandre is merely a secondary character in *Les Météores* (*VP*, 250). Yet since he also maintains that the reader collaborates with the writer and that the author must respect the audience's creative participation in the novel's meaning (*V*, 7–12), the reader's reaction cannot be discounted.

To a great extent the problem of where the novel's center lies stems from the fact that *Les Météores* began as another book. The original title was to be *Le Vent Paraclet* (*The holy spirit*) and, as Tournier explains: "My initial project aimed at a resacralization of heavenly phenomena through a fusion of theology and meteorology, the one bringing the spirit, the divine and the sacred, while the other the very concrete poetry of the rain, the snow and the sun. The point was to efface the difference between the two meanings of the word sky: *air, atmosphere,* and *abode of God and the blessed,* and then to rejoin the sun cult sketched in *Vendredi"* (*VP,* 252). What actually happened, perhaps mercifully, was something different: "In truth the novel developed in a much more profane sense. The sacred only appears in a sporadic fashion. The research that I did . . . (on various theological matters) . . . did not lead to the fictional development I was seeking" (*VP,* 253).

The difference of opinion among the author, some critics, and many readers comes mostly from the novel's long germination and the various changes it underwent in the process. Tournier started with one book in his head and ended up with another. The readers, not apprised at the time of publication of the author's intentions, and having only the text, gravitated toward a character whose passion for the concrete contrasted sharply with the often obscure ruminations of the super-intellectual Paul. One might argue that Paul is the greater mind, but Alexandre is certainly the more striking fictional creation.[4]

Whether or not Tournier intended it, *Les Météores* is the final installment of a trilogy (*Vendredi* and *Le Roi des Aulnes* are the other two) whose principal theme is the struggle to create some form of order amid the chaos of human experience. *Les Météores* constantly reflects backwards on the two other works. Allusions to Robinson Crusoe abound and Abel Tiffauges makes a brief but significant appearance. In *Les Météores* both Alexandre and Paul (who is his brother Jean's perfect twin) set out to order their universes. Alexandre knows that his creation is an arbitrary, self-indulgent fantasy, while Paul remains convinced of the objective truth of his discoveries.

Viewpoints

Les Météores begins with an extensive description of weather conditions along the English channel on 25 September 1937. Several persons are mentioned in passing, but they do not reappear. Prominent among them is Michel Tournier, who is reading Aristotle's *The Meteors* on the beach at Saint-Jacut.

The opening passages of *Les Météores* constitute a modest parody of the beginning of Robert Musil's *Der Mann ohne Eigenschaf-ten* (The Man without Qualities). This literary game has no great significance for the novel, but it does indicate something of *Les Météores* stylistic complexity, if not preciosity.[5] The story is not complicated, but the telling of it is.

Tournier employs a constantly shifting narrative perspective. At times he uses a seemingly omniscient narrator, but then he will switch to the points of view of Paul, Jean, Alexandre, Sophie (for a brief time Jean's fiancée), and Shonin, a Japanese expert on gardens.

An added problem is the time perspective. Whereas Alexandre, Sophie, and Shonin tell their stories at particular moments in the novel and indicate no knowledge of the future or of what the others are saying, Jean and Paul enjoy a broader perspective. Jean obviously has access to some of Paul's writings since he comments on them.[6] Paul has even a greater advantage. Early in the story *Les Météores* (*M,* 62) Paul refers to an injury he sustained in the novel's penultimate chapter. This indicates that Paul's version of what transpires is entirely retrospective, that each time he describes an incident or comments upon it, he does so with the fullest available knowledge of what finally occurred. If this is indeed the case, then Paul's narration ought to be the most credible, since it would be the most inclusive. Yet in *Les Météores* Jean's perspective on the events serves only to underscore the weakness of the interpretations Paul gives to them.

The Story

Shortly after World War I Edouard Surin married Maria-Barbara who rapidly proved herself to be a model of fecundity. At regular nine-month intervals she would produce a child. Eventually she gave birth to twins whose resemblance was so total that people began to mask their confusion concerning which was which by referring to them collectively as Jean-Paul. The twins did everything together; they even slept in the same bed, locked one to the other in complimentary fetal positions. They also had their own language, aeolian, which was incomprehensible to everyone except a retarded boy and themselves. While Jean and Paul adored their mother and liked their philandering, fun-loving father, they had no use for their legion of brothers and sisters, each of whom they indifferently referred to as "Peter."

Maria-Barbara and her brood lived in a little town in Brittany, Pierres Sonnantes, where Edouard is the titular head of a mattress factory. Next door was a home for retarded children, Sainte-Brigitte, that was presided over by the kindly Sister Beatrice aided primarily by a laconic Nepalese nun, Sister Gotama. One of the more severely disturbed children, Franz, managed to gain national attention by displaying an uncanny ability to provide instantaneously the exact day of the week for any possible date: "What day will be 4 July 42930?—A Monday" (*M,* 58). Only Jean and Paul were able to communicate with Franz, who understood their special language, aeolian, but not even the brothers' solicitude was enough to prevent the boy from drowning himself.

Alexandre Surin is Edouard's younger brother. When a ridiculous accident takes the life of their pious older brother, Gustave, Alexandre inherits the responsibility for supervising one of the family's businesses: the removal and processing of garbage. To the family's general astonishment, Alexandre proves to be extremely adept at this line of work. He is in fact quite proud of the six dumps he controls, proud enough to have medallions made, one for every dump. In each medallion he places a representative particle of the dump's content. Alexandre, the self-styled "dandy of sewage," is never without these medallions, and in times of stress he is prone to use their contents as snuff.

When Alexandre was a student at a boarding school, Le Thabor, he belonged to a band of homosexuals who called themselves *"les Fleurets"* ("the foils"). Principal among them was Thomas Koussek who likes to make love to a life-size statue of Christ on the cross. Later, as an adult, Alexandre runs into Thomas who has become a Catholic priest. Together they engage in a complicated discussion of the Holy Spirit, *"le Vent Paraclet."*

Despite their perfect physical similarity, the twins develop very different personalities. Paul is sure of himself, willful and imperious, while Jean is open, nervous, and curious (*M,* 10). Although Paul is perfectly happy to live his life with Jean at Pierres Sonnantes, Jean wants to explore the world, break free from what Paul terms their "perfect cell of twinship," and even marry. Paul thwarts this latter effort when Jean foolishly brings his fiancée, Sophie, to Pierres Sonnantes.

The Pierres Sonnantes that Sophie visits is a place deprived of the maternal presence of Maria-Barbara and the numerous, nameless Peters. The brothers and sisters have all left to pursue their insignificant lives, but the fate of Maria-Barbara is tragic. During World War II, Maria-Barbara, unknown to all, became the leader of a Resistance group. Not even Edouard knew of her activities, and one evening when the Gestapo arrived to arrest her, the foolish, good-hearted Edouard supposed that his modest, anti-Nazi activities in Paris had been discovered and his moment of ultimate heroism had finally arrived. But the Gestapo were only interested in Maria-Barbara; she is the one they send off into the night and fog of Buchenwald, never to be heard of again. After the war Edouard attempts to find a trace of his wife. In despair at his fruitless efforts and broken by illness, he weakens and dies.

After Sophie's precipitate departure from Pierres Sonnantes (she made love to Paul thinking he was Jean), Jean deserts his brother and, inspired by Jules Verne's *Around the World in Eighty Days,* sets out on an extensive voyage with Paul in pursuit. The chase is told almost entirely from Paul's perspective. The first stop is Venice, but then Paul procedes to North Africa, to a place he terms the Island of the Lotuseaters which is the home of an Anglo-American couple, Deborah and Ralph. From there he goes to Iceland, Japan, Canada, and finally Berlin where the infamous Wall is in the process of being constructed. In an attempt to get out of East Berlin and rejoin Jean, Paul undertakes a hazardous trip through a dark, wet tunnel. Paul is halfway through when an explosion rocks the tunnel and maims him horribly.

Alexandre also does a great deal of traveling. This is partly due to his business obligations, his need to oversee the workings of the various dumps, but it is also the result of his pursuit of various young men. A large portion of the sections Alexandre narrates consists of his commentaries on the evils of heterosexual society, the correlation between homosexuality and genius, the superiority of the artificial over the real, the social function of garbage dumps (they constitute a sort of museum of Western civilization), and the general stupidity of humankind. Alexandre's best friend turns out to be a homosexual dog whom he names Sam because he found him on Saturday, *samedi,* but not even Sam's companionship is permanent. Alexandre loses Sam during the Nazi takeover of Paris, and in one of the novel's most touching moments, Alexandre first experiences the ugliness of Nazism when he witnesses the arrival at the Paris dump of thousands of dead animals. It is worth noting in passing that Tournier, like other novelists who treat World War II such as Céline, Günter Grass, and Siegfried Lenz, finds that the most artistically effective way of depicting Nazi butchery is through the description of slaughtered animals.

Alexandre Surin's travels ultimately take him to Casablanca where, aging and saddened by the death of a young lover and for the first time in his life disinterested in finding a new one, he permits himself to be killed in an easily forseeable ambush.

At the novel's end Jean is nowhere to be found, Edouard, Maria-Barbara, and Alexandre are dead, and Sainte-Brigitte, the home for retarded children, has been closed. Paul is a crippled recluse at Pierres Sonnantes, but his final reflections remain nevertheless positive. He fancies that he has absorbed his brother's identity into himself, that vegetation is somehow sprouting from his broken body, and that he is secure in his understanding of himself and his universe. Paul's last word, which is the novel's as well, is "Sublimation."

The Ordering of Things

Les Météores is Tournier's most intricate book. It is hardly surprising that in a novel that includes Tournier's most elaborate depiction of twinship, dualities abound. Scenes frequently parallel and parody one another as, for example, when a nun's speculation concerning the language of her retarded charges points to Paul's more arcane reflections about aeolian. Also, practically every character is in some measure the mirror image of another personage in the novel. Yet what matters in all the dualities and parallels is that the most obvious one, Jean and Paul, is really not very important.

Although a major portion of *Les Météores* concerns Paul's pursuit of Jean, Jean is not as significant as he first appears. Jean chooses life in all its unstructured complexity, a fact that Paul acknowledges when he states that his brother "is seduced by irrationality" (*M*, 152). For Jean the issue is quite simple; he "wants to tear up the fraternal pact" and "live, finally live" (*M*, 238). Jean's desire to live his life without worrying about controlling every aspect of it makes him similar to Vendredi, and in *Les Météores* he plays a role that resembles that of Robinson's savage. Jean, like Vendredi, is less important in himself than in the way he clarifies the personality of the man who tries to dominate him. In terms of the thematic development of twinship and order in *Les Météores*, the tension between Jean and Paul serves as a catalyst for Paul whose thoughts and actions assume enormous importance while his brother literally fades out of the novel. The real clash over the meaning of twinship and the need for order concerns two men who are fascinated by both, Paul and Alexandre Surin.

Tournier's great champions of order—Robinson, Abel Tiffauges, and Paul—share three important attributes. The first is their common fear of madness. It is partly to suppress this anxiety that Paul chases Jean around the world (*M*, 425). Their second shared characteristic helps balance this fear: the conviction they are somehow participants in a special destiny and thus superior to their fellows. Paul states this quite bluntly: "For a longtime I have considered myself a superman. I still think that I have an uncommon vocation" (*M*, 156). The third attribute is by far the most important, but also perhaps the most dangerous: all three are convinced (Abel loses his confidence at the end of *Le Roi des Aulnes*) that the various orderings of experience that they discover do indeed exist in reality. *Les Météores*, more than any other of Tournier's novels, explodes this fantasy.

Paul

Paul Surin is the intellectual center of *Les Météores*. His reflections set the tone, and the actions and thoughts of the other characters are best understood as implicit commentaries upon, and occasionally parodies of, Paul's intellectual comportment. In this respect Tournier is certainly correct when he describes Alexandre as a secondary character.

With more insistence and intensity than either Robinson or Abel, Paul maintains that the ordered universe he inhabits conforms to reality. Even at the end of the novel, after an incredible series of reverses and enormous physical suffering, he can say, as Abel was prone to announce in the early sections of *Le Roi des Aulnes:* "everything is a sign" (*M,* 54). Jean is perceptive when he says of his brother: "Paul is the man of all the plenitudes, of all the fidelities." The key word here is "fidelities," and what Paul is most faithful to is the basis of his ordered universe, the concept of perfect twinship. Paul is certain that he shares with Jean a unique experience and a special language that set them above the rest of mankind. When they are united in their "twin cell" they lack for nothing and nobody.

Paul, in an exaggerated version of the twin myth found in Plato's *Symposium,* believes that the rest of the world is attempting to achieve by artificial means the wholeness that is the privilege of perfect twins. Paul shares with his uncle Alexandre a contempt for heterosexuals, "les sans-pareils" ("those without equals") whose lovemaking practices he finds disgusting. For homosexual couples he has a degree of respect mingled with scorn. Homosexuals try to form a "twin cell," but the result is always artificial because "the homosexual is a *without equal,* he cannot deny it" (*M,* 335). Nonetheless, the homosexual, in his efforts to achieve perfect twinship, is not without qualities: "The homosexual is an artist, an inventor, a creator. In struggling against his unavoidable unhappiness, he occasionally produces masterpieces in all areas" (*M,* 336). It is otherwise for perfect twins: "The twin couple is at the opposite extreme from this creative and wandering liberty. Its destiny is fixed forever . . . it does not know how to move, suffer or create" (*M,* 336). According to Paul, theirs is a state of perpetual Nirvana, a quasi-permanent existence within the womb.

If Paul has any doubts about his superiority, they emerge rarely and briefly. At one point he does muse that "twinship is an affair of conviction" (*M,* 141), but this possible hesitation is offset by an amazing assertion: "when I consider my past, I cannot doubt the existence of an invisible, omnipotent presence of this principle (perfect twinship), to the point that I wonder whether—with the exception of mythological couples like Castor and Pollux, Remus and Romulus, etc.—Jean and myself are the only true twins who have ever existed" (*M,* 141–42). For Paul, even if no other twins have achieved the state of perfection

that he ascribes to his brother and himself, what he says about
Jean and his twinship remains incontravertibly true.

Paul fails to see, or chooses not to see, that the perfection
he envisions has little to do with life as it is actually lived.
What he describes is a prenatal state of being. At the beginning
of the novel the omniscient narrator associates the closeness
of Jean-Paul with their physical proximity to Maria-Barbara: "In
truth everything that separated them from each other separated
them from their mother" (M, 10). When Paul and Jean are
united in their interlocking fetal positions they are striving to
re-create the wholeness, warmth, and safety of the womb, an
impossible goal and one that is no less artificial and impermanent
than the efforts of homosexual lovers to achieve the "twin cell."
The futility of Paul's attempt to maintain his womblike existence
with Jean becomes cruelly apparent in Berlin. When Paul begins
his ill-fated journey through the tunnel, he is obviously reenter-
ing a womb, but a womb that rejects him horribly and leaves
him deformed and bereft forever of his brother's presence.

The tunnel scene is the most dramatic illustration of the futility
of Paul's aspirations, but it is not the only example. The story
of the retarded boy-genius, Franz, told partly by the narrator
and partly by Paul himself, provides a striking analogue to Paul's
situation. Franz is a mixture of brilliance and debility (M, 57).
He cannot function outside the womblike atmosphere of Sainte-
Brigitte and is terrified by any unexpected occurrence. Yet he
has an obsession with calendars; he loves the control over time
that his knowledge of days and dates provides. Paul reflects
this mania for controlling time when he travels across Canada.
He minutely details the arrival times at the various stops and
their distance from his goal, Montreal. Paul does touch upon
the similarities between the twins and Franz when he notes
that only they can converse with Franz in their secret language,
aeolian, and he even remarks that, like Franz, he fears changes
(M, 63). Yet Paul never really examines the parallel between
Franz and himself, a parallel so glaringly evident that Paul's
description of Franz resembles himself at the end of Les Météores:
"he had fled the company of his equals into himself, barricaded
in a fortress of silence and refusal. . . ." (M, 61). This parallel
is all the more striking when one recalls that Paul tells his story

retrospectively, with a full knowledge of all that has transpired, from his wheelchair at Pierres Sonnantes.

Another parallel that eludes Paul involves the alcoholic American, Ralph, who with his wife Deborah has created a heterosexual version of the "twin cell" in North Africa. Over the course of many years and with considerable labor Deborah wrested from the sandy soil a beautiful garden and created for her husband and herself an idyllic world that is described as the island of the Lotuseaters. But tragedy occurs even in this paradise of forgetfulness when cancer claims Deborah's life. As Deborah is dying a powerful storm destroys the garden and a few hours later Ralph is left without a wife and without the comfort of the beautiful surroundings. It is at this juncture that Paul meets Ralph and describes him as follows: "he refused the reality of the situation and only saw what he wanted to see" (*M,* 415). Deborah was Ralph's Jean and, in the face of her loss, all he can do is cling to a pathetic fantasy. Paul duly notes this, but draws no inferences that might pertain to his own situation.

At the end of *Les Météores* Paul claims victory. Seated on the beach at Pierres Sonnantes he regards the ocean as he senses his body taking root in the earth around him. Jean, he remains convinced, has been absorbed into himself and so the perfect twin cell is once again united. Calmly he watches the falling snow: "Above the mass of hard snow trembles a transparent fog. The snow becomes vapor without melting, without sinking, without softening. That is called sublimation" (*M,* 542). This description serves for Paul as well. He remains at the end unchanged and unbending, convinced of his personal superiority and of the perfection of his world. Yet the cost of this happiness is enormous sublimation, enormous enough to be akin to madness.

Alexandre

Paul and Alexandre Surin never speak in *Les Météores.* Nonetheless, the novel is an extended dialogue between them with Paul taking the lead and Alexandre's thoughts and acts comprising a commentary on his nephew's main theme: the ordering of experience. Alexandre wants to be able to control life too,

but instinctively he understands something that Paul never
grasps: that all order is necessarily artificial. Perhaps the greatest
irony in *Les Météores* is that the outrageous and shocking Alexandre Surin is, along with Maria-Barbara, one of the sanest persons
in the novel.

The source of Alexandre's sanity is his genuine self-knowledge. Unlike Paul he can truly examine himself and his relationship to the world around him. Early in the novel he remarks
that "I have constructed a universe for myself, perhaps a mad
one, but one that is coherent and resembles me . . ." (*M,* 34).
When Alexandre mentions "madness" in this context he is not
expressing some deep-seated fear. He is merely attesting to a
fact that is obvious to him: his world is a product of his fantasy
and as such quite fragile (*M,* 35).

Alexandre makes no attempt to have his world conform to
reality. For him "reality" is in a philosophical sense largely
unknowable, but what constitutes its ugly equivalent in daily
life are the ethical and sexual norms of bourgeois society. Alexandre's stupid and pious brother Gustave embodied one form
of social respectability until three tons of garbage landing on
his head jolted him out of complacency and into oblivion. A
more dangerous example of socially acceptable conduct is offered to Alexandre by Adolph Hitler who, to the cheers of
the German populace, proposes making the world a better place
by ridding it of Jews and homosexuals. Alexandre considers
both of these men to be fools, but dangerous ones, since the
particular fantasies they espouse are shared by millions of "right-
thinking" people in the world.

Alexandre responds to the stupidity of middle-class standards
by creating his own values and life-style. However bizarre Alexandre's world may appear, it has one quality in common with
bourgeois society: its tenets are arbitrary and artificial. Alexandre
does consciously what society does unconsciously; he capri-
ciously determines some standards of conduct and then adheres
to them rigorously. What is most inventive about Alexandre's
values is their willful deviation from the "natural." Take his
taste in food: "I love food that is elaborately prepared, sophisti-
cated, and unrecognizable. . . . I have a weakness for the
alimentary transvestite. For mushrooms, those vegetables disguised as meat, for sheep's brains, that meat disguised as fruit

pulp, for the avocado whose thick flesh resembles butter, and more than anything else I like fish whose false flesh is nothing, people say, without the sauce" (*M*, 82). His taste in everything runs toward the artificial and the "contrary to nature," because he understands that what passes for natural is most often the result of an arbitrary choice and definition.

Thomas Mann once defined art as a very serious joke. This same description, applied to life rather than art, appears to reflect Alexandre's viewpoint. In his home Alexandre prefers furniture that is at least an imitation of an original or, at best, an imitation of an imitation. The more removed from some traditionally established criterion of originality, the better he likes it.

Alexandre extends this notion to the realm of thought: "The idea is worth more than the thing, and the idea of the idea more than the idea" (*M*, 86). What Alexandre enjoys about abstraction is its creative aspect. Since nothing has any inherent significance, any interpretation is possible and the more fascinating the assigned meaning is, the more pleasurable and exciting life becomes. On an intellectual level this is Alexandre's equivalent of Paul's "sublimation," with the important difference that the uncle, unlike the nephew, knows that it is all make-believe.

Alexandre appreciates the meanings that others supply to their experience, provided that their interpretations do him no harm. The only woman who intrigues him is Fabienne de Ribeauvillé, a lesbian who decides to marry a fop named Alexis de Bastie d'Urfé because his name and demeanor remind her of a character from *L'Astrée,* Honoré d'Urfé's seventeenth-century novel. In this seemingly endless novel, about three thousand pages in all, Céladon is the somewhat effeminate swain who loves Astrée and whom circumstances compel to pass much of his time disguised as a shepherdess. Alexandre is much impressed by the complicated game that Fabienne plays: "This witch Fabienne would be capable of marrying either a woman or a man whom she would have first of all decked out in a bridal dress and veil. She is stronger than I am. Like Sam (his homosexual dog), she scandalizes and enriches me. Her remarks are cynical and edifying" (*M*, 223).

Another person whose fantasies Alexandre admires is his old schoolboy companion and fellow homosexual Thomas Koussek. The Thomas who at school was enamoured of the crucified

body of Christ has become a Catholic priest whose lust for Jesus
has yielded to his adoration of the Holy Spirit. While the two
dine together in a rectory (the food is unrecognizable), Thomas
offers a complicated theory of the *ruah,* the holy wind which
he believes figures prominently in the cosmic scheme of things.
Yet the details of the theory matter less[7] than the way that
Thomas's appreciation of the Holy Spirit has permitted him
to live a happy life.

Not surprisingly, Alexandre's most elaborate example of in-
venting meanings involves himself. On an inspection tour of
his dump in Roanne he finds himself in a situation where he
can be two people at once. He meets an attractive worker named
Eustache Lafille. Alexandre is struck by this odd name, especially
because in French slang Eustache and Surin (Alexandre's surname) both mean "wicked knife." His passion is further aroused
when he learns that Eustache has a young and beautiful friend
named Daniel. If Eustache (the prey) originally excited Alexandre, Daniel (the prey of the prey) becomes an even more interesting conquest. When Alexandre first came to Roanne he took
a room in the best hotel, the Terminus, where he was the respect-
able, middle-class M. Alexandre Surin. In order to better pursue
Daniel, Alexandre also rents a room in a dilapidated workers'
lodging called the Rendez-Vous des Grutiers (the Meeting Place
of Crane Drivers) where he is known as Monsieur Alexandre,
and then in a touch that he enjoys, as M. Surin Alexandre.
Thus, in this boring little town Alexandre can act out two different roles, something he does with enthusiasm and describes
with hyperbole. After a brief sojourn in Paris he is overjoyed
to return to Roanne: "I came back to my two hotels . . . with
the satisfaction of Ulysses returned to Ithaca after the Trojan
War and the Odyssey" (*M,* 175).

Like Paul, Alexandre wants to maintain a tight control over
his life and the world he inhabits. Unlike Paul, he can recognize
the inevitable moment when that control escapes him. Daniel
dies a horrible death on the day that World War II breaks
out. He is torn to pieces by rats as he tries to cross a dump
to rejoin Alexandre. "The dandy of sewage" realizes that his
lover's death is to some extent his fault. Saddened by Daniel's
death and then by the disappearance of his beloved Sam, Alexandre begins to lose his taste for life and the structuring games

that made it worthwhile. He lives out the war, further embittered by the knowledge that this is but one more stupid conflict among the many that bourgeois society is determined to experience. On a visit to his dump in Casablanca Alexandre consciously decides to enter into a dangerous situation. He follows a boy through the darkened port streets and dies fighting in a totally expected ambush. Alexandre has played enough with life and, once his enthusiasm began to wane, he decided to depart in a final, dramatic exit.

The Homosexual as Vigilante

Many readers of *Les Météores* were shocked by Alexandre's flagrant homosexuality and his constant abuse of heterosexuals. In the two earlier novels, Tournier shrouded questions of sexual identity in ambiguity. Robinson says that he has no sexual desire for Vendredi, that he had acceded to a higher level of sexual awareness. Abel's *phorie* was intended as a sexual experience that did not fall into either the homosexual or heterosexual category. Such subtle distinctions are meaningless to Alexandre Surin; his sexual proclivities are clearly fixed and accentuated by his dislike for most women and all heterosexual men. Nevertheless, in terms of *Les Météores*'s development what matters is not the relative virtues of the "gay" and the "straight" worlds. In each of Tournier's first three novels the sexual orientation of the hero has been different from the norm, and in these three cases, including *Les Météores,* Tournier is using these differences to provide a basis for social criticism.

Sexual practices that deviate in any way from the socially accepted norm create a degree of alienation for the individual concerned. A person who discovers that his or her sexual preferences are different from the majority is compelled to examine a part of his or her being that people with allegedly natural inclinations have no cause to consider. Now as *Vendredi* and *Le Roi des Aulnes* illustrate, sexual identity is a more complex issue than most people care to appreciate. In these first two novels the ambiguity of sexual desire was paramount, but in both cases the heroes could recognize that they were different and each strove, with varying success, to come to grips with this difference. This is not Alexandre's situation. He knows what he is and accepts it. His function is not to make people aware of how complex sexuality is, but to expose first of all the danger entailed by an unexamined acceptance of heterosexuality as the unique form of sexual expression. However, the basic issue goes beyond sexuality. Alexandre detests middle-class complacency in all its manifestations. For him there is no social norm that ought not to be questioned; they are all artificial and serve to encourage people not to think. Heterosexuality raised to the level of an absolute value is one barrier among many to honest self-examination. Alexandre's alienation from the mass of society, an alienation directly related to his sexual identity, gives him a perspective that is clearer than most. He understands, for instance, that despite the assurances of churchmen and politicians, none of society's values is fixed and eternal. They are in fact continuously altered and created by whoever happens to be leading the state. And as Alexandre reflects upon the times in which he lives this question of leadership is hardly academic: "I recognized him at once, the Greatest Heterosexual, the Chancellor of the Reich, Adolph Heterosexual, that brown devil who destroyed in his camps of horror all of my brothers whom he trapped in his claws" (M, 294).

Alexandre exaggerates, he is nasty and unfair, he prefers shocking to explaining, but even given his numerous faults he does perceive the great menace that threatens Europe. The rats' claws that destroyed Daniel were only a modest foreshadowing of Hitler's ability to tear apart. Yet most people do not appreciate the danger that Hitler presents because they have convinced themselves that he is the enemy of marginal individuals, deviates who have nothing in common with themselves. What these good citizens fail to understand, and what obsesses Alexandre, is that from a madman's perspective everyone is in some measure a member of an offending social class: "Stupid bastards! How can you not know that once he takes the first step [against homosexuals], the tyrant will attack another elite minority. He'll send to the slaughterhouse priests, professors, writers, Jews, union heads . . ." (M, 103). Alexandre is of course correct, but his knowledge does him little good. With Alexandre Surin, Michel Tournier would appear to suggest that if the trauma of sexual difference can lead to a more accurate understanding of society's workings, the insights thus attained will remain unheeded by most people.

Robinson's Heritage

No matter how one chooses to interpret *Les Météores,* there is no way of avoiding the two preceding novels. Tournier alludes to *Vendredi* and *Le Roi des Aulnes* throughout the novel. A minor character, Urs Kraus, physically and tempermentally resembles Abel, "a sweet giant" and lives in a modest hotel on Robson-strasse (*M,* 477). Abel Tiffauges makes a brief appearance in *Les Météores* when he carries Jean on his shoulders during a carnival, and both Sister Béatrice and Thomas Koussek speak of limbo, thus recalling the subtitle of *Vendredi, "The limbo of the Pacific."*

These allusions are not mere literary games. *Les Météores* is the culmination of a discussion that dominated the other two novels as well. It concerns the need for, and the possibility of achieving, a perfectly coherent ordering of human experience. While *Les Météores* certainly attests to this need, both its own story and the continuous references to the other novels indicate how limited are the chances of creating such a perfection in this life.

Robinson is the only truly happy man in the three novels. However, his happiness, the triumph he experiences at the novel's end, is due mostly to his isolation on the island. Robinson is an adult whom circumstances permit to live in a world of childlike simplicity. Although he can reenter Speranza's cave he has no desire, unlike Paul, to return permanently to the womb. Robinson is an interloper in limbo who profits from his good fortune.

Les Météores makes clear that if limbo exists in the twentieth century, it is only for children and mad people, and even then the environment must be strictly controlled. The kindly Sister Béatrice is convinced that the idiocy of her charges does nothing more than reflect the fact that these poor children were created for another and better world, "limbo perhaps, a place of innocence" (*M,* 52). Thomas Koussek associates the end of limbo with the beginning of adolescence and the entry of himself and

the other *Fleurets* into boarding school: "leaving the limbo of
infancy, we were opening our eyes on a new world" (*M,* 124).
What remains significant here is that limbo (childhood) is a
state that must be left behind in the modern world. A contemporary Robinson is simply impossible and that is the tragedy of
Franz.

Franz represents a modern effort to re-create Robinson Crusoe. Paul speaks of him in terms that recall Robinson's situation
and aims: "He fled the company of his fellows into the interior
of himself, barricaded in a fortress of silence and refusal, trembling and crouching at the bottom of his cave" (*M,* 61). Whereas
Tournier's Robinson does manage to protect himself against
others and eventually even conquer his fears, Franz fails in his
efforts.

One of the most famous scenes in Defoe's *Robinson Crusoe*
occurs when the overconfident Crusoe takes a small boat too
far out to sea and is almost lost. As previously mentioned, in
Defoe's religious allegory this represents Crusoe's not having
yet conquered his pride. He attempts to go too far too quickly
and the result is near disaster. Crusoe does, however, survive
this test and, like Tournier's Robinson, he does surmount the
various crises that beset him, but Franz has no such luck. He
too sets out in a small boat with a crew of Down's syndrome
children and all of them drown (*M,* 70–72).

Paul, whose sense of others is often more accurate than his
understanding of himself, offers a succinct commentary on Abel
Tiffauges. Paul watches with horror as Abel places Jean upon
his shoulders: "This man is a slave, and not only a slave, but
an assassin" (*M,* 169). As cruel as these words are, they contain
a modicum of truth. In *Le Roi des Aulnes* Abel becomes a slave
to a misunderstood destiny and his acts, quite aside from his
intentions, lead to the deaths of numerous adolescent boys.
Abel's effort to assert total control over his life end, as do Franz's,
in disaster.

When Paul claims that Robinson lives in a dream world (*M,*
365), his words are harsh but accurate. What Paul does not
appreciate is that Robinson's isolation allows him to live out
his life in that dreamworld. No matter how unreal is Robinson's
situation on his island, he is still able to achieve genuine happiness there. Alexandre appears to understand this when, sad-

dened by the loss of Sam, he ruefully remarks: "Robinson's desert island was more welcoming and teeming with friends than my garbage desert!" (*M*, 290).

The perfection of Robinson's dreamworld is not attainable in the twentieth century unless one attempts to re-create the isolation from human contact and conflicting opinions that he managed on his island. Paul certainly tries, but Pierres Sonnantes is no Speranza; it is a place where sublimation masks despair.

Chapter Five
Le Coq de bruyère

A Collection

Le Coq de bruyère is a collection of thirteen short stories and Tournier's one play, *Le Fétichiste* (The fetishist). Tournier wrote these pieces at different times and for differing purposes. "Amandine ou les deux jardins" (Amandine or the two gardens) was done originally as a children's tale; "La Mère Noel" (Mother Christmas) and "La fugue du petit Poucet" (The escapade of little Poucet) are Christmas stories; and versions of "Le Coq de bruyère" (The grouse), "L'Aire du Muguet" (The lily of the valley field), and "Les suaires de Véronique" (Veronica's shroud) have appeared on French television. *Le Fétichiste* has been staged in Berlin and Paris. When asked why he entitled this volume *Le Coq de bruyère,* Tournier responded simply that "Le Coq de bruyère" was the longest story in the collection.[1]

There is no compelling reason for a group of short stories to have any underlying motifs. A writer might group his shorter works together in one volume just to sell more books. While Tournier is doubtless interested in the financial success of his writings, this present collection is far from being a literary potpourri. Although the stories and the play range in subject matter from the creation of the world ("La Famille Adam") to the travails of contemporary truck drivers ("L'Aire du Muguet"), they all have two things in common. One is the reiteration, amid radically different settings, of the themes that have characterized the three earlier novels. The second concerns the underlying purpose of *Le Coq de bruyère.*

Tournier chose as an epigraph for this collection some verses of Lanza del Vasto:

> Au fond de chaque chose, un poisson nage.
> Poisson de peur que tu n'en sortes nu,
> Je te jetterai mon manteau d'images.

> At the bottom of everything a fish swims.
> Fish, lest you emerge naked,
> I will throw you my coat of images.

On the backcover of *Le Coq de bruyère* Tournier explains his reasons for choosing these lines: "These verses . . . define in a few words the work's entire aesthetic. Just like birds in the bushes or crabs under rocks, some truths lie in wait under our most familiar objects, silenced by the tongues of people we meet every day. These truths are often subtle, difficult, sometimes frightening, hideous, and magnificent. It is the role of the metaphysician to display them in their terrible and incomprehensible nakedness. It is the task of the storyteller to clothe them appropriately and to make them dance to the music they have within themselves."

Michel Tournier, "métaphysicien manqué" and "conteur par préférence," attempts in the play and the stories to expose the mysterious qualities of human existence, sometimes sad, sometimes funny, that are hidden behind the banality of everyday life. It is to this end that he occasionally retells a story so famous and well-known that it has become something of a cliché. Tournier parodies Bible stories ("La Famille Adam"); he completes famous novels ("La Fin de Robinson" [Robinson's end]); and he offers modern versions of beloved stories ("La fugue du petit Poucet" is a contemporary rendering of a seventeenth-century story, Charles Perrault's "Le petit Poucet"). Tournier plays with famous musical motifs as well. "Que ma joie demeure" (Let my joy last) and "La jeune fille et la mort" (Death and the maiden) refer to compositions by J. S. Bach and Franz Schubert respectively. In an interview published the year that *Le Coq de bruyère* appeared (1978), Tournier mentioned that his short stories (*contes*) have a quality that "will wound the natural logic of things."[2] A sense of the irrational and the mysterious permeates all the works in this volume and contributes to the vitality of the individual works as well as to the overall effect of *Le Coq de bruyère*.

To speak of the underlying unity of themes and purpose in *Le Coq de bruyère* in no way implies that everything in the collection is of equal value or complexity. Some of the stories, like "La Mère Noël," have a simple loveliness that an extensive analysis would in no way enhance. The force of another story, "Tupic," resides entirely in its shocking ending whose vividness requires no explanation. Also, since the effect of *Le Coq de bruyère* is culminative and stems from the reiteration and variation of Tournier's obsessive themes, it seems unnecessary to discuss each work in detail. A wiser course would be to show how Tournier develops his thematic concerns throughout the various stories and the play and then choose one piece that appears to sum up the principal elements in the collection. That work would be "L'Aire du Muguet."

Themes

In the three earlier novels certain motifs were clearly predominant. Time and again Tournier returned to his obsession with order, the complexity of sexuality, especially sexual identity, the Cain and Abel personalities, the intermingling of reality and fantasy, truth and fiction, and perfect twinship. Except for the issue of perfect twinship, all the other motifs appear in *Le Coq de bruyère.*

Order. Jehovah creates the order in "La Famille Adam," but, as is typical in Tournier's writing, the order escapes even the Creator. Despite Jehovah's intentions Adam manages to get himself expelled from Paradise and then fades out of the story. The real hero is Cain whom his brother Abel provokes. Cain kills Abel, but it is really not this act that enflames Jehovah against him. What He dislikes in his grandson is that Cain, like Himself, delights in ordering experience. Abel, his favorite, presented no such difficulties; he just enjoyed wandering about, at ease in a chaotic universe. The problem is that events justify Cain's pretensions. The order he creates is modest, but effective; at first it consists of well-tended fields, but after Abel's death forces him to flee, Cain's inveterately sedentary nature leads him to found the first city which he names after his son: "Hénoch was a city of dreams, shaded by eucalyptus trees. It was simply an expanse of flowers where at the same time the voices of fountains and turtle doves cooed."[3] Along with the Robinson of *Vendredi,* Cain is one of the most successful of Tournier's orderers. Cain's needs are simple; he stakes out and controls a little bit of the world. Ultimately even Jehovah attests to his grandson's wisdom when, after years of traveling with Abel's sons, he returns to Cain's city and allows himself, after some grumbling for the record, to be taken in and worshipped by the family of Cain.

The Robinson of "La Fin de Robinson" at first appears to be more Defoe's than Tournier's. He has left the island to return to England, where he married and became wealthy. But this Robinson is plagued by discontent. Like the young girl in "La jeune fille et la mort" whose perpetual ennui leads her to fantasies about the joys of death, Robinson is bored by the world around him. Against all advice and what passes for good sense, he sets out to rediscover his island. In vain. He returns to England, an aged drunkard who can only mutter that the island is "Un-find-able" (*C,* 23). One evening in a tavern an old helmsman explains to Robinson that the island is right before him. He has simply not recognized it: "She's gotten old, just like you. . . . Just go look in a mirror" (*C,* 24). Robinson looks and he sees the island. He has always carried it with him because this place of idealized beauty was always his creation, a creation that was the mirror of his state of mind. The passing years have altered Robinson's body and aspirations and his island has in turn reflected that change. Yet more than physical strength and beauty, what time has robbed Robinson of is the gift of imagination.

Lucien Gagneron is the dwarf in "Le Nain rouge" (The red dwarf). For years he had tried to pass himself off as a short man by wearing elevator shoes. As such he was an object of scorn for men and of sexual ridicule for women. Then one day he suddenly finds himself, through a variety of circumstances, naked before the beautiful Edith Watson who is fascinated by the idea and later the reality of a dwarf lover. It is at this moment of sexual conquest that Lucien discovers his true vocation. He is an actor who puts some order into his life by playing the role of a dwarf. Like Alexandre Surin, Lucien appreciates that all orderings of experience are artificial and temporary and so the goal is to invent the ones that provide the greatest pleasure. Edith does not love Lucien Gagneron the dwarf anymore than she could have loved Lucien the short man; she is responding to the image of the dwarf as a sexual giant. After Lucien murders Edith because she is about to reconcile with her estranged husband, Bob, Lucien joins a circus where his thespian gifts develop fully. Here he receives the love and respect which the daily world denied Lucien, the short man.

Eventually Lucien works Bob into the act and plays David to Bob's Goliath and then Neron to Bob's Agrippina. Lucien's greatest moment as an actor, and the moment when he most controls his world, occurs on Christmas Eve when he insists that only children be admitted to the circus. Surrounded by people even tinier than himself he plays the role of the red dwarf, but what he is actually doing is acting out a fantasy where he is king amid his adoring subjects. Lucien Gagneron, who in the real world is a murderer, a liar, an exploiter of the oafish Bob, achieves in the dreamworld he has created for himself, the right to be "honored by his people" (C, 110).

If Lucien Gagneron is an artist, he is a cynical one. He understands the limits of his fantasies and does not attempt to overstep them. In "Les suaires de Véronique" Véronique is a serious artist, a photographer, whose goals are more elaborate and dangerous than Lucien's. In pursuit of artistic perfection she slowly destroys her young model Hector. She makes him cover his body with a photographic fluid and then she wraps him in photosensitive sheets that capture the boy's form while they deprive him of his identity. Although the story's title recalls the New Testament legend of Veronica's veil, the true inspiration is the Old Testament injunction against graven images. Just as Paul Surin believed that he had absorbed his brother Jean's identity, Véronique thinks she is transforming Hector's transient, physical existence into an immortal work of art. The New Testament's legendary Veronica perserved on her veil Christ's face for eternity, but the Hector that Véronique captures is unrecognizable, "a cadaver in a winding sheet" (C, 157). Véronique's desire for control has done little except turn her into a "witch" (C, 156).

In Tournier's world the best ways to order experience is to fall upon very special and fortuitous circumstances (Robinson), have modest goals (Cain), consciously act out carefully circumscribed fantasies (Lucien), or simply acknowledge that any ordering will be artificial (Alexandre Surin). The main character in "Tristan Vox" starts out with a fairly clear understanding of his one gift. Felix Robinet (Felix Faucet) is a ridiculously named actor who throughout a long career (he is over sixty) has enjoyed only a modest success. A simple man from the Auvergne whose great love is the heavy food of that region, he nonetheless possesses a mellifluous voice that suddenly charms thousands of radio listeners. Felix's stage name is Tristan Vox. In the story the persona that Felix creates takes on a greater reality than his creator. To Felix's horror and confusion both his wife and secretary, among countless others, fall in love with Tristan and no amount of sensible talk can alter their feelings. As the story ends, Felix stands numbly by as his wife persists in writing love letters to the dashing Tristan Vox. The fantasy world he has created for his wife and others has become so fulfilling that the truth of the matter is no longer of any importance.

Martin is the fetishist. Like other Tournier characters, notably Abel Tiffauges and Paul Surin, he considers himself a "man of destiny" (*C*, 284), who can assure himself and anyone else that "nothing was my fault" (*C*, 283). Women's underwear fascinates Martin; he believes that possessing lingerie gives him a control over a woman that is on a higher level than the physical. When he steals a girl's bra he is convinced that he now has her essence, "the key to her being" (*C*, 296). While a number of Tournier's characters find it necessary to insist that they are indeed sane (Robinson, Abel, Paul), Martin is the only one whom society commits to an asylum. This is not because his conduct is more deviant than the other characters. It is just that his tensions, his inability to cope with daily existence, manifest themselves more flagrantly. Martin is the most obvious example in Tournier of a person who wants total control over his universe without having to enter into normal contact with other human beings. If Paul Surin rejected life by attempting to reenter the womb, Martin's refusal of life is more melodramatic and frightening: "I'm coming back [to the asylum]. With my flag. The black flag of pirates. Long live death" (*C*, 302).

Sexual identity.   "La Mère Noel" is essentially a sermon that illustrates with the simplicity that befits the genre, the ambiguity of sexual identity. The village of Pouldreuzic is divided between the clerical and the anticlerical camp. When the divorced Mme Oiselin becomes the new school teacher speculation runs rife concerning her religious beliefs or lack of same.

The issue comes to a head on Christmas Eve, since the believers traditionally flock to midnight mass while the anticlericals have Santa Claus (Père Noel) distribute presents to the children. The person who plays Santa Claus is usually the school teacher. Mme Oiselin extracts herself nicely from this dilemma. She volunteers her infant son for the role of the baby Jesus at mass and she gives out the presents to the nonbelievers as Mère Noel. All goes well until baby Jesus gets hungry and starts to cry. Once again Mme Oiselin masters the situation. She enters the church dressed as Santa Claus and on the altar, in the midst of mass, she gives her breast to the hungry child.

This story has no complexity. It gently shows, in a way well-suited to impress children, that rigid distinctions between male and female roles impoverish one's understanding of human nature. A more complicated development of this theme is "Amandine ou les deux jardins," subtitled "un conte initiatique" (an initiation story). Amandine is a young girl on the verge of puberty who loves her family's well-tended garden and her cat, Claude. Her initiation begins when Claude gives birth to kittens. (There is a little joke here that might elude English-speaking readers. Although Amandine assumed that Claude was a male, in French "Claude" is an androgynous name.) Amandine's family manages to find homes for all of the kittens except one, Kamicha, who stays with his mother. Kamicha leaves the family garden and lives on the other side of the wall in a wild, overgrown garden. Amandine observes that Kamicha appears to have two separate and distinct identities, one for each garden. In the family garden he is timid, while on the other side of the world he is calm and self-assured. One day Amandine decides to climb the wall and visit the other garden. Its lushness and disorder thrills and frightens her: "I want to cry and I'm happy" (C, 42). In this strange garden she notices the statue of a winged boy that impresses her without her knowing why. Later, back in the "garden of her childhood" (C, 43), she notices some blood spots on her leg. Now it suddenly occurs to Amandine that she looks a bit like the boy in the statue.

With this story, written originally for children, Tournier seems to suggest that the passage from childhood to incipient maturity is not a discovery of one's maleness or femaleness. It is the discovery of both.

Charles Perrault's "Le petit Poucet" is one of his most famous stories. It concerns a poor couple with seven sons whom they cannot feed. In desperation the parents try to lose their boys in the woods, but the cleverness of the youngest, little Poucet, saves the brothers. However, on another occasion not even Poucet can find the way out of the forest. In their wanderings the brothers stumble upon the house of an ogre who resolves to eat them in the morning. Poucet manages to trick the ogre into killing his own daughters while he and his brothers flee. The ogre chases the boys wearing boots that allow him to travel seven leagues in a bound, but once again Poucet outwits him. The youngest brother steals the boots, defeats the ogre, and along with his family lives happily ever after. In some verses at the story's end, Perrault clearly states the moral: sometimes the weakest can also be the smartest and eventually the most famous.

This is not the lesson Tournier draws in "La fugue du petit Poucet." The story is set in a Paris of the future where Poucet's father, a woodcutter charged with supervising the removal of all the trees in Paris, instructs his son and cringing wife in the virtues of modernity. They live in a high-rise apartment where the windows need not open since the air conditioning provides the daily quota of fresh air and the insulation deadens the roar of the jets that pass just above. Poucet runs away on Christmas Eve. He gets lost in the woods, but is discovered by the seven daughters of M. Logre (*l'ogre* is French for "the ogre"). This ogre is a hero, an excellent, kindly father whom his children adore. Logre is just the opposite of Poucet's supermasculine, narrow-minded father. He does the sort of housework tradition-ally assigned to women and possesses a sort of beauty that amazes Poucet: "Vous êtes beau comme une femme" ("You are hand-some like a woman" [*C,* 55]), he says. Logre belongs to what is fashionably termed the counterculture. He smokes dope with his children and offers a version of the Fall that is not canonical. According to Logre Adam did not err in eating of the Tree of Knowledge since it opened his mind to the complexity of good and evil. The villain in this account is Yahweh, the estab-lishment figure, who wanted to keep Adam ignorant and preju-diced, just like Poucet's father. The next morning, Christmas Day, the police arrive accompanied by M. Poucet. They arrest

Logre, but before being carted off to jail Logre gives Poucet magic boots that allow him to escape the confines of his dreadful apartment and fly about the world. On these trips he can become whatever he pleases.

In "La fugue du petit Poucet" the boy's admiration for Logre's combination of male and female qualities frees him to live a fuller and richer life. He will no longer be bound by the sorts of values that limit a person to develop only one side of his personality. As the story ends Poucet can even imagine himself a vast chestnut tree (*C*, 61).

Tupic, the main character in the story that bears his name, is less fortunate. Like Poucet, Tupic finds his father's aggressive masculinity abhorrent, but unlike the other child, he has no mentor to guide him. Tupic senses, as does Poucet after Logre's version of the Fall, that life is not really the way his parents have described it to him. This occurs when the boy makes the puzzling discovery that in paintings that depict the triumph of the saved and the torture of the damned, the lost souls appear strong and God's chosen weak. Even more disturbing to him is society's insistence that because he is a boy he must become a man. This general social truth is vividly illustrated to the child's mind by the fact that in the park where he plays he can only use the boy's toilet and never the girl's. The portals to these two restrooms are guarded by a woman that Tournier rather unsubtly compares to Cerberus (*C*, 70). Tupic is further confused when he learns that a boy he played with is actually a girl and thus has the right to enter the room forbidden to him. Eventually he comes to understand that what prevents him using the other toilet is his phallus and in the final scene, as predictable as it is horrible, he attempts to solve the problem by cutting off the offending member. Tupic, incomplete as a boy, but unable to explore being a girl, ends up as neither.

Cain and Abel.   The Cain and Abel motif figures in a number of the stories in *Le Coq de bruyère*. The most obvious example is in "La famille Adam," but in this instance there is an interesting variation. In most of Tournier's earlier works the character who was predominantly an Abel personality tended to be the more positive figure. Abel Tiffauges is infinitely more human than the enigmatic Nestor and Jean is certainly more appealing than Paul. This changes in "La famille Adam," where Abel's nomadic tendencies reflect a brutal and selfish temperament. In this story the work of civilization, which in the end even Jehovah deems valuable, is Cain's work.

"Le Nain rouge" develops the Cain/Abel motif still more. Both Bob and Lucien have at various moments the qualities of a Cain and an Abel. What is implicit in all of Tournier's writings, that each person has Cain and Abel aspects to his personality, is made perfectly explicit in this story.

In two other places in *Le Coq de bruyère* Tournier varies this technique of intermingling Cain and Abel qualities in a single personality. In both cases the Cain/Abel dichotomy signals the sublime and ridiculous sides of an individual. The main character in "Que sa joie demeure" is named Raphael Bidoche. Raphael recalls the great painter and points to the great talent for the piano that Tournier's Raphael possesses. "Bidoche" in French slang means a morsel of old, tough meat. This part of the name underscores the fact that Raphael has sacrificed his concert ability to make a living as a clowning pianist. Felix Robinet in "Tristan Vox" has a similar sort of name. In Latin Felix means "lucky" and that reflects his success on the radio, while the Robinet (Faucet) surname attests to the resolute banality of his true personality. In these two characters it would be silly to argue over which part of the name indicates the Cain or the Abel personality. What matters is that the names indicate the existence of contradictory tendencies within the same individual.

Reality and fantasy. In almost all the stories in *Le Coq de bruyère* the line between reality and fantasy, truth and fiction is narrow to nonexistent. One could claim that in "Tristan Vox" the only reality is the pure fantasy created by the radio voice. When Felix enters his tiny studio and the red light signaling the show's start goes on, he is like a man "buried in a sort of tomb" (*C,* 123). But what emerges from this tomb is something much greater and more real than Felix Robinet. It is a veritable Resurrection: "Tristan Vox resounded like an omnipresent God in everyone's ears. He entered their hearts and spread out like the Phoenix in their imaginations" (*C,* 123).

Imagination does not function in a vacuum. To take a modest example, little Poucet's ability to see an elephant and a Christmas tree in the form of a moving truck (*C,* 52) is to some degree the result of the stories he has read or heard. Social values represent a potentially more insidious source of human fantasies. Baron Guillaume Geoffrey Etienne Hervé de Saint-Fursy is totally defined by the traditions of his caste. He loves horses, fencing, women, and witty conversation in approximately that order. He is the "coq de bruyère": "People called him affectionately 'the grouse' ['le coq de bruyère'] because of his talk, and also for his arched calves and constantly jutting chest" (*C,* 189).

The story begins in the autumn of the baron's life. He is still an excellent fencer, horseman, and good conversationalist, but he is undeniably old. His wife seems almost grateful for his advancing years because they have seriously curtailed his philandering. When a young girl who reminds him of the actress who starred in "Barbe-bleue" ("Blue Beard," a story by Perrault and already alluded to in *Le Roi des Aulnes*) comes to work for his wife, the baron embarks on what he knows will be his last fling. His success with Mariette is quick and predictable.

After the baron establishes the girl in a little apartment on the other side of town, his wife unaccountably begins to go blind. The baron, true to his code of honor, immediately abandons Mariette to stay at his wife's side. The baroness' sight then begins to return. Enraged by what he judges to be dishonesty on his wife's part, the baron attempts to renew his liaison with Mariette, but it is too late. The girl runs off with a younger man, the baron has a stroke, and in the last scene Tournier describes the baroness pushing her paralyzed husband in a wheelchair. All that Guillaume Geoffrey Etienne Hervé de Saint-Fursy can mumble is, "le bonheur parfait" ("perfect happiness" [*C,* 189]).

As "le Coq de bruyère" opens the baron is fencing with a young officer whom he easily defeats. The audience is impressed by the baron's fencing skill, but then somewhat taken aback when he removes his mask and they see how old he is. This little scene encapsulates the baron's character and situation. He has imprisoned himself in a series of social masks which hide from himself and others the person he really is. His values, which he takes to be those of a well-adjusted adult, are actually an amalgam of socially encouraged fantasies about eternal youth, honor, and sexual attractiveness. The baron plays the role he believes a baron is supposed to play. His interest in Mariette is more than a tribute to her youth and beauty; she is the sort

of girl he is supposed to seduce. Likewise, when his wife falls
ill, the baron's role demands that he comport himself in a certain
way, that of the noble, self-denying husband. The baron could
have been happy as Don Juan or the Good Samaritan, but not
as both at the same time. When the baroness recovers her sight,
the baron considers her guilty of somehow not playing her role,
and he finds himself in a situation where he has no social model
to emulate. He is stripped of his masks and left with no identity.

However imperfect or even silly were the baron's masks,
they did serve the useful purpose of protecting him from boredom. It is precisely the fear of boredom that haunts Mélanie,
the young heroine of "La jeune fille et la mort." As a child
the taste of lemons provided her with some titillation. Later
she tried making love to a social inferior, but to Mélanie death
itself always seemed the most exciting experience. Throughout
the story she plans her death elaborately, at various moments
fantasizing about the joys of hanging, suicide, and poisoned
mushrooms. When an old man makes her a present of a minia-
ture guillotine, Melanie finally decides. The doctor who examines her corpse is puzzled by his own diagnosis: Mélanie died
of laughter.

Mélanie's laughter and the baron's "le bonheur parfait" are
both examples of "le rire blanc" ("white laughter"), the discovery of the absolute meaninglessness of human existence. This
experience can occur when fantasies that have coddled a person
no longer function, and all that is left is a sense of the sheer
stupidity of everybody and everything. Death or a form of insan-
ity might well follow, since in Tournier's universe life without
fantasy is no life at all.

"L'aire du Muguet." More than any other story in *Le
Coq de bruyère* "L'aire du Muguet" brings together the principal
motifs that have permeated Tournier's writing up to this point.
Pierre is a young truckdriver who lives on a tight and inflexible
schedule. His mother awakens him early, he eats in haste, and
before dawn he is in his beloved truck on his way to pick up
his co-driver, Gaston. Together they set out for Lyons where
they drop off one load, spend the night, and with a new cargo
return to Paris the next day. The route never varies. When
leaving Paris the pair always take their morning break in a
field just off the highway, "l'aire du muguet." One day Pierre

sees a girl in the field tending cows. He begins to see her regularly on their periodic stops and in one conversation she mentions that she lives in a little village called Lusigny-sur-Ouche which is a half kilometer from the highway.

On his next trip Pierre makes an uncharacteristic detour. Despite Gaston's protests he drives the truck off the highway and onto a backroad where he searches in vain for Lusigny-sur-Ouche. In the course of his increasingly frenzied attempts to find the village Pierre knocks over a war memorial and a crucifix. Eventually Gaston takes charge of the truck and manages to get it back on the highway, but the next morning when they are again passing "l'aire du muguet" Pierre suddenly stops the truck. He jumps out of the cab and tries to cross the highway to get to the field. Despite speeding motorists' efforts to avoid him, Pierre is hit by several cars and grievously injured. The ambulance that carries the delirious Pierre to the hospital pulls off the highway and races past a little sign: "Lusigny-sur-Ouche, 0.5 km."

In one of the first scenes of "L'aire du Muguet" Pierre is kneeling before his truck. His ostensible purpose is to clean it, but the obvious symbol is one of worship. Pierre adores his truck for the sense of order and control it provides. He enjoys sitting in the cab, perched above the world, and at one point he confides to Gaston that in a truck "you dominate" (C, 245).

Pierre's love for the truck extends to the highway as well. In France there are two principal categories of roadways, the A roads and the N roads. A roads are main highways (autoroutes) and N roads are smaller, local roads (nationales). Pierre prefers the A roads because they are straight and clean; they lead to their destinations without any deviations. The A represents Pierre's idealized notion of life, and the truck is the symbol of how he wants to pass through life. He wants to remain above life's complexities, observing everything, but from a safe distance. Pierre says that when he was a child, he thought things were more beautiful in shops, where they were enclosed behind windows and thus untouchable. As an adult, Pierre's attitude remains much the same: "The windshield is like a store window. Look at the countryside through it. Well arranged and impossible to touch. Maybe that's why it's more beautiful" (C, 258).

This is Pierre's simplistic version of Alexandre Surin's: "The idea is more than the thing, and the idea of the idea more than the idea" (*M*, 86).

Distance also contributes to Pierre's sense of control. When he talks to the girl he is separated from her by a barbed wire fence, and even when he dances with her to the music of a Viennese waltz, the fence remains between them. Unlike the adolescent Amandine, Pierre cannot successfully cross a barrier that in fact divides one part of himself from the other. The reason is that for all his efforts, he does not really want to open himself to experience. As the ambulance takes him to the hospital, he murmurs, "you know, when you're on the *A* road, you shouldn't try to get off it" (*C*, 270–71).

Pierre's sexual repression is one aspect of his desire to control and simplify his life. He fears the risks that attend passion. Gaston senses his friend's innocence and great capacity for error (*C*, 242). As is typical of Tournier's heroes, when Pierre loses control the results will be chaos. The *N* roads represent all that is complicated and mysterious in life, and it is no surprise that while Pierre frequents the *A* roads during the day, it is at night that he ventures onto the *N* roads. His frantic search for Lusigny-sur-Ouche involves the destruction of all the barriers he has erected against life. During this trip he encounters an assortment of odd, seemingly mad people who make his quest for the elusive Lusigny and the girl all the more difficult. The destruction of the war memorial and the roadside cross suggest Pierre's total break with traditional forms of religious and secular authority. This nightmarish journey is truly into the heart of darkness.

Pierre says that he is a man of the *A* roads whereas Gaston is made for the *N* roads. Together these two men constitute the most interesting Cain and Abel couple in the collection, with Pierre being essentially a Cain personality who succumbs to his Abel tendencies and Gaston an Abel who has come to appreciate the value of the Cain within himself. Gaston does not really like the *N* roads, but he can travel them. His life has been varied and he has permitted himself to be changed by his experiences. As a youth Gaston engaged in the Resistance only to emerge disillusioned by what he saw and did. He married, but his life as a truckdriver involved frequent absences

from home and this led to a divorce. In the past he had eaten
and drunk too much, but now is extremely careful about his
health. Gaston has the simple good sense of someone who has
profited from what he has done. In this respect he resembles
the Cain of "La famille Adam." Pierre is similar to the Adam
of that story since behind his amiable facade he has many unexamined tensions that lead him to extreme and dangerous acts.
When Gaston tells Pierre that highways and women do not
mix (C, 252), he is merely reflecting on his failed marriage,
but in the larger context his words suggests the incompatibility
of total control and passion.

The night world that Pierre enters is a milieu where reality
and fantasy intermingle. Lusigny-sur-Ouche is only a half kilometer from the road, but he can never find it. As he speeds around
the darkened roads, things become increasingly unreal. People
do not respond to his questions, he knocks over the cross and
the monument with apparent indifference, and scuffles with a
bunch of masked adolescents. Gaston becomes so exasperated
that he begins to wonder whether either the girl or the village
actually exists (C, 268). The sign at the end of the story assures
the reader that the village is real and in the daylight Gaston
had seen the girl. However, whether the girl or the town that
Pierre had in his head were real remains a moot point.

Le Coq de bruyère appears to mark the end of one period of
Tournier's artistic development. With the publication of this
collection and the reiteration of themes that have characterized
his earlier novels, Tournier seems to exhaust a certain line of
inquiry. There are some variations in *Le Coq de bruyère* (the
slight development of the Cain-Abel motif is the best example),
but generally speaking these stories do not venture into previously explored realms. This will be the task of *Gaspard, Melchior
et Balthazar.*

Chapter Six
Gaspard, Melchior et Balthazar

Tournier and Religion

The publication of *Gaspard, Melchior et Balthazar* led to a controversy over Tournier's religious beliefs. The author himself
claimed that *Gaspard, Melchior et Balthazar* marked his attempt
to write "a Christian novel,"[1] and he further announced that
shortly before its publication he had sought an *imprimatur* from
the bishop of Versailles.[2] Critics immediately began to wonder
whether he had converted to some orthodox form of Christianity. Tournier fueled this sort of speculation through a series
of provocative and even shocking comments. In one interview
he noted that while he belonged to no religion, Christianity
was his personal ideal.[3] These sentiments were certainly encour-
aging to Christians anxious for a potential convert, but then
on another occasion, after reiterating that Christianity was good,
Tournier went on to suggest that the Roman Catholic church
was bad because of its "profound hatred of life."[4] He particularly
regretted that the contemporary church was no longer perse-
cuted. He even wondered whether impaling a few priests and
burning several nuns would not help renew the faith.[5]

Such sentiments did little to endear Tournier to believers,
and their annoyance was doubtless increased by his rather self-
serving foray into scriptual exegesis. It is true that the famous
gifts of the Three Magi, gold, frankincense, and myrrh, have
proved a treasure house for religious interpretation, but no one
found such personal implications as did Tournier: "I only desire
three things: gold, frankincense and myrrh. Gold represents
the author's profits, frankincense, good critical reviews, and
myrrh is eternal fame."[6]

Now a French author who earlier in his career could suggest
it was a pity that the Germans did not burn down Paris, is no
stranger to controversy, not to mention publicity. It is therefore

tempting to dismiss as sheer provocation Tournier's reflections
on religion and its role in his life. Yet this would be a mistake.
Tournier's interest in religion antedates by far the publication
of *Gaspard, Melchior et Balthazar,* and theological issues have
figured prominently in all of his novels, especially *Les Météores.*

In *Les Météores* Thomas Koussek adumbrates a theory of the
Holy Spirit that lies at the center of Tournier's religious thought
but which is not fully developed until *Gaspard, Melchior et Balthazar.* At dinner with Alexandre Surin, Thomas describes his spiritual growth. What stands out from the beginning is that Thomas,
unlike other Tournier characters, was seeking a means of ordering experience that stemmed from something other than his
personal fantasies. As a young man he easily reconciled his homosexuality and love for Jesus by sleeping with a life-size statue
of the crucified Savior. Later, after becoming a Catholic priest,
Thomas realized that this particular way of making sense out
of his life was inadequate because it was at once too fantastic
and too literal—too fantastic because it was excessively controlled by his sexual reveries and too literal because it paid
too much attention to the person of Christ.

Thomas's reflections took him beyond Jesus and toward *l'Esprit* ("the Spirit") whose original manifestation was a sacred
wind, the *ruah* which "indicates something vast, ample, open,
but also an odor, a perfume. It is also sometimes a slight contact,
a soft caress, a feeling of well-being wherein one bathes" (*M,*
135).

In the Christian era the *ruah* achieved its highest expression
in *l'Esprit,* a word Thomas believes has traditionally been given
a too ethereal definition. For Koussek *l'Esprit* never loses its
concreteness; it is "wind, tempest, breath, it has a meteorological
body" (*M,* 136). When Tournier has Koussek say that in relation
to *l'Esprit,* "the meteors are sacred" (*M,* 136), the author seems
to be alluding to Aristotle's description of meteors: "their provi-
dence is everything that happens naturally, but with regularity."[7]
L'Esprit passes over and through all aspects of experience and
sanctifies everything it touches. *L'Esprit* proclaims that life's fear-
ful complexity is nothing other than one aspect of its richness.
However, the fear that most human beings have of life's richness
compels them to invent false distinctions which frustrate them
and impoverish their existences.

The most radical aspect of Thomas Koussek's theology of *l'Esprit* was that it moved beyond the Christ figure. In Tournier's latest novel, his idiosyncratic version of the journey of the Magi, Jesus never really appears. The book manages to address religious topics without engaging in complicated theological discussions; yet at the same time it reflects much better than his interviews or occasional comments what Tournier values in Christianity. *Gaspard, Melchior et Balthazar* deals with four men's efforts to discover who they are, and then to accept what they find.

Three Magi Plus One

Most of *Gaspard, Melchior et Balthazar* concerns the stories of the three kings, and the final and longest single section treats a fourth king, Taor, who manages to arrive late for both the Nativity and the Last Supper. The middle sections of the novel consist of two fairy tales, "Barbedor" (Golden beard) and "L'Ane et le Boeuf" (The donkey and the ox), and King Herod's grim discussion of his life and times.

Gaspard. Gaspard is the black king of Méroé. One day his astrologer informs him that a comet, in the shape of a golden head, is passing through the skies, an omen that bodes ill for the kingdom and the king. Shortly thereafter Gaspard notices in the slave market two blond slaves, apparently brother and sister, and on a whim he buys them. In time he falls in love with the blond girl, Biltine, and as a result begins to feel ashamed of his blackness. Gaspard's self-esteem diminishes with each day and reaches its nadir when he discovers that the brother and sister pair are actually lovers who have been exploiting him. Uncertain about what to do, Gaspard imprisons the offending couple and sets out on a voyage that eventually takes him to Bethlehem.

Gaspard's spirits improve somewhat when, at the tombs of Adam and Eve, he starts to wonder whether Adam was perhaps black. But it is the visit to Bethlehem that restores his shattered self-respect. The infant that Gaspard sees in the manger is black.

Balthazar. Balthazar is king of Nippur. He is an aging aesthete who has devoted his life to the quest for beautiful objects, especially Grecian artifacts. In Nippur Balthazar has constructed a museum, the Balthazareum, where he displays the treasures he has collected in the course of his numerous travels. During one such trip he receives the shocking news that his fanatical high priest has incited a riot in his absence and provoked a mob to destroy the Balthazareum. The king is disturbed not merely at the loss of his art works; he is troubled as well by the priest's absolute conviction that art is essentially profane and constitutes an insult to God and religion. In Bethlehem Balthazar's anxieties are assuaged. He learns that God cannot disapprove of graven images since any depiction of the world is a tribute to the beauty of Divine Creation. Rather than being profane, art is indeed sacred.

Balthazar resolves to reconstruct the Balthazareum, but he will no longer fill it with works from the past. Henceforth he will only have works (paintings and sculptures) that celebrate his own age and the experiences of his generation. The first painting that Balthazar commissions is a portrait of the Three Magi.

Melchior.   Melchior was supposed to become king of Palmyrène, but immediately after his father's mysterious death the prince is overthrown by his unscrupulous uncle. Forced to flee his own country, Melchior wanders to Jerusalem where he meets Gaspard and Balthazar. The two kings befriend the destitute prince and when they go to Herod's palace, Melchior accompanies them dressed as a servant. Herod quickly makes clear that he knows who Melchior is and in fact knows nearly everything about Balthazar and Gaspard as well.

Herod offers his guests a dinner of unrivaled opulence, but one which his various illnesses prevent his eating. To amuse himself and the others Herod has a servant tell a story. This is "Barbedor," a fairytale about an elderly king who loses his beautiful beard strand by strand. The king eventually discovers that each day during his siesta a strange bird plucks one hair. The king pursues the bird and in the course of his chase he becomes a child again. At the story's end the little boy returns to the palace to find the old king (his former self) being buried and himself proclaimed the new king.

Herod enjoys this tale because it is so removed from his own experience of kingship. His story is one of ceaseless deceit, murder, and constantly shifting alliances. From all the sordid details of his life Herod draws one lesson: evil is necessary to gain and retain political power.

Melchior leaves Herod's palace disillusioned and confused. He no longer possesses a strong desire to win back his throne, but he is equally uncertain about what he wants to do with his life. It is only at Bethlehem that he discovers that the kingdom which best suits him is not of this world. Melchior, his soul at peace after having seen the Christ Child, decides to become an anchorite.

A donkey named Kadi Chouia describes the Nativity. After recounting the difficulty of his life and the confusion reigning in Bethlehem, the animal tells of the people and the angel who were present at the birth.

Taor. There is no fourth Magus in the Gospels, but were it not for the invention of Taor, prince of Mangalore, Tournier might never have written his novel: "I was working, in effect, for a year on my kings. As can happen, I ran into some problems and had to abandon the project for a time. One day, I was listening, by chance, to a German radio station. During the broadcast the writer Edzard Schaper spoke of the fourth king, the one who left too late, who missed the encounter in Bethlehem and was condemned to wander. That day I discovered my novel. The fourth king was my true starting point."[8]

Prince Taor is a fop. His great passion is candy, and one day a servant offers him a morsel of "rahat loukoum à la pistache," ("pistachio Turkish delight"). He loves this sweet and wants the recipe. Taor sends out messengers to learn the secret, but they return empty-handed. However, they do tell him the stories they have heard of a Great Confectioner who knows how to make a candy that surpasses any other. After a great preparation and accompanied by an elaborate entourage, Taor sets out in quest of the great man.

The voyage proves long and costly and the prince misses the Nativity at Bethlehem. He nonetheless manages to meet the other kings and learns both of the happiness they have found in Bethlehem and of their hesitation to report the Child's birth to Herod. The others leave, but Taor decides to have a big party for the children over two years old who live in the area. It is during this festivity that Herod's soldiers sweep down on the village and destroy all the male children under two years

old. Taor is horrified, but he also has the obscure sense that
he is now beginning to discover the nature of his destiny.

The prince continues his journey despite the advice of his
chief counselor. Eventually he comes upon the city of the Sodomites, a world of salt and darkness and as such at the antipodes
of everything this spoiled youth of sweetness and light had ever
cherished. Taor frees his servants to go their way and all depart
except for his accountant who wants the prince to sign a letter
that frees the man from any financial responsibility for what
has happened. Taor readily acquiesces, but first he tries to buy
the freedom of a poor man accused of stealing thirty-three
drachmas. He offers to pay the man's debt, but when his funds
prove insufficient, Taor volunteers to take the prisoner's place
in the salt mines. He stays there, mostly underground, for thirty-
three years.

Taor emerges at the end of his sentence an old, broken, and
starving man. While in prison he encountered a baker who
gave him the recipe for pistachio Turkish delight, but this sweet
no longer holds any charm for him. More significant was his
meeting with a prisoner that had witnessed the preaching of
one Jesus Christ whose sermon on a mountain makes a great
impression on Taor. It is because of Jesus' words of comfort
that Taor sets out—following his release—to find Him in Jerusalem. Once again he arrives too late. The famished Taor does
stumble on the remains of the Last Supper which he immediately
begins to devour. What follows is the most beautiful passage
in the book and the novel's last words: "Taor got dizzy: bread
and wine! He reached for the cup and raised it to his lips.
Then he gathered up a piece of unleavened bread and ate it.
He rocked forward but did not fall. The two angels who had
been watching over him since his release gathered him up in
their vast wings and, as the night sky opened up with a great
light, they carried off the one who, after having been the last,
the perpetual latecomer, had just been the first to receive the
Eucharist."[9]

A New Order

All of Tournier's previous works attest to a need for order.
In each case order meant some means of simplifying experience

since, appearances to the contrary, what characterizes a Tournier hero is fear of complexity. *Gaspard, Melchior et Balthazar* constitutes a new stage in Tournier's work precisely because it celebrates complexity.

The main characters in this novel are all tortured by false contradictions and artificial dichotomies. "I am black, but I am king" (*G*, 9), are the words of Gaspard that open the novel. Melchior laments that "I am king, but I am poor" (*G*, 83), and Balthazar suffers because his love of physical beauty puts him at odds with his nation's religious leader.

Tournier's earlier heroes might have resolved these problems by a dramatic, albeit arbitrary decision. They might have chosen blackness over kingship, or the flesh over the spirit. In *Gaspard, Melchior et Balthazar*, however, there are no such facile solutions. In fact this novel does more than develop Tournier's ideas, it parodies some of his earlier concerns. For instance, there are references throughout to "sedentary nomads" (*G*, 34), and "sedentary voyagers" (*G*, 69), but these expressions are no longer replete with ominous allusions to Cains and Abels; they merely describe the way life brings out contradictory qualities in an individual. In a similar vein Gaspard exposes the potential for self-delusion that can attend the search for mythic prototypes. This occurs when he casually remarks that legends are only valuable when one cooperates with them (*G*, 44). In *Gaspard, Melchior et Balthazar* there is little cooperation with arbitrary orderings of experience.

In Bethlehem the three kings discover that the contradictions that plague them are merely apparent. Gaspard's racial shame dissolves as he gazes at the black Christ Child (this is the only physical description of Jesus in the novel), and Melchior learns that there are kingdoms to rule that require no earthly riches. Balthazar perceives that terrestrial beauty is nothing other than an emanation of God's ineffable splendor and so to love what the world offers and what artists create is a means of worshipping the Divine Creator of all. Yet aside from each king's personal revelation, the fundamental illumination of Bethlehem is that the Godhead, the Supreme Orderer, is an amalgam of seemingly insoluble contradictions: "this Heir to the Kingdom mingled incomparable attributes, greatness and smallness, power and innocence, plenitude and poverty" (*G*, 150).

In Michel Tournier's novels the complexity of creation frightens as much as it fascinates, and human suffering often results
from the inability to accept the richness of the universe. What
the Magi learn is not to live with contradiction, but to acknowledge that many of the dilemmas that people experience are
forms of self-torture that stem from their own imaginings. What
provokes the Slaughter of the Innocents and damns Herod is
not what the king thinks: "I am king . . . but I am old" (G,
122). His error, and it is typical of Tournier's heroes, is to
insist that life conform to his narrow vision of it. Herod cannot
accept human destiny and understand that transience is part
of the Eternal Plan.

The story of the three kings marks the culmination of the
reflections on ordering experience that have characterized Tournier's writings from the beginning. Tournier uses the fourth
king, Taor, for other purposes.

Tournier and Christianity

Through the invention of the king who loved candy Tournier
was able to come to terms with Christianity. Taor's voyage is
the reverse of that of his fellow kings. He departs in a state
of perfect harmony and plunges into a world of contradiction.
His quest for a sweet leads him from his sun-filled land into
the darkened city of the Sodomites.

If the other kings had to struggle to accept what they were,
Taor had to learn an opposite lesson. Namely, that what he
was at the outset—an indolent, pampered heir to a throne—
was not the limit of what he could be. The Magi started and
stopped before he did; for them the revelation of Christ was
sufficient. For Taor, a disciple centuries before his time of Thomas Koussek, Christ would not be enough.

Taor is the first person to receive the Eucharist. According
to the Roman Catholic church, the process by which ordinary
bread and wine become the Eucharist, the Body and Blood of
Christ, is called transubstantiation. This means that while the
bread is no longer bread and the wine no longer wine, these
two elements maintain their usual physical appearance. The doc-
trine of the Eucharist, this transformation of the physical into
the divine without the loss of physicality, is the Christian notion

most compatible with Tournier's own thinking: "I believe I have a sense of the sacred . . . I live in the absolute, in a world totally vertical where each being like a tree plunges into the depths of the mud, and, in the same movement, reaches toward the most ethereal heights."[10]

Tournier altered the story of the Last Supper by making Taor the first communicant, and kept Christ in the background throughout the novel because what interested him was not the particular facts and dogmatic niceties of Christianity. What Tournier discovered in transubstantiation is the confirmation of his belief in transformation: that everything which exists, be it as humble as bread and wine, has the potential to become sacred, and this process occurs when people learn to perceive themselves and the objects that surround them as sources of comfort and joy. Tournier was not fooling when he stated that *Gaspard, Melchior et Balthazar* "will be my *Salammbô.*"[11] While the differences between these two novels are easily ascertained, they share— and Tournier's comment alludes to this—a celebration of the lushness of the universe.

Tournier's religious sensibility calls to mind the pantheism of Spinoza, the philosopher he claims to follow. Throughout his career Tournier has insisted upon his philosophical orientation: "One must not forget that I come from philosophy"[12] and in *Le Vent Paraclet* he mentions that Spinoza's *Ethics* "is the most important book which exists after the Gospels" (*VP,* 299). Yet what separates Tournier from the pantheism that Spinoza espoused is that the former's position is never as rigorously developed as the latter's. Tournier, the philosopher of the sacred, yields to Tournier the novelist who becomes ill at ease when the elaboration of abstract principles moves him too far from the concrete: "I cannot disembody the sacred and push it into the realm of the abstract."[13] It may be useful to recall here that Tournier's *Esprit,* which traverses the world, transforming and sanctifying all it touches, is eternally "filled with semen."

Tournier and Huysmans

Shortly after the publication of *Gaspard, Melchior et Balthazar* Tournier referred to himself as "the Huysmans . . . of my generation"[14] and termed his writing "mystical naturalism,"[15] an expression sometimes used to describe certain of Huysmans novels.

Joris-Karl Huysmans (1848–1902) began his literary career as a disciple of Emile Zola and his early works, *Marthe* (1876) and *Les Soeurs Vatard* (1879), show the influence of naturalism. These novels emphasize, in great and sordid detail, the struggles and numerous frustrations of the lowest social classes.

Huysmans was undistinguished as a naturalist and did not achieve fame until the publication of *A Rebours* (*Against the Grain,* 1884) and later *Là-Bas* (*Down There,* 1891). These works are products of Huysmans "decadent" period where he indulged his tastes for dilettantism, satanism, the pursuit of artificial paradises, and the study of medieval culture. What followed was a conversion to Roman Catholicism and the writing of several religious novels. Huysmans died a Benedictine oblate.

"Mystical naturalism" (also called "spiritual naturalism") is a loosely used term sometimes applied to *Là-Bas* and Huysmans's subsequent religious fiction. It refers to a mingling of vivid, minute descriptions of the immediate surroundings with a quest for, or at least a belief in, a spiritual reality. This is essentially what Tournier understands by a *conte:*

I write *contes* [stories]. The *conte* is opposed on one hand to the nouvella and on the other to the fable. It is opposed to the nouvella in the sense that the nouvella does not say anything: it is just a slice of life which expresses a philosophy that life is quite ugly and sad. In contrast, the moral of the fable is written in black and white. As for the *conte,* it has qualities of the other two. I mean by that that in the *conte* there is a significance, but nobody knows what it is; I would say that the *conte* is a nouvella haunted by a meaning, like having a ghost in a house; but one never learns what exactly this meaning is. . . .[15]

Since from the beginning of his career Tournier has insisted that he writes *contes,* stories anchored firmly in the real world, but with ambivalent implications that make them more than a slice of life or a tale with an explicit message, "mystical naturalism" marks no new development in his literary style.

Tournier's relation to Huysmans and the decadent tradition is a more complicated question. If the world is, as Tournier says, filled with keys and keyholes,[17] it remains nonetheless important not to force the locks. He is no more a true decadent that he is a consistent Spinozist, although any reader of his autobiography and fiction can find numerous reasons to place him in a decadent context. Certainly, an artist who relates that he lives in a former rectory, who delights in arcane knowledge, who puzzles over the differences, real or imagined, between the natural and unnatural realms, and whose religious references tend to emphasize the aesthetic dimension, particularly of Roman Catholicism ("the gold, the incense, and the organ respond to the need for jubilation that is in our heart" [*VP,* 60]), would appear to be a contemporary Des Esseintes, the main character in *A Rebours.* Also, the shadow of Gilles de Rais, which hovers over Abel Tiffauges in *Le Roi des Aulnes,* conjures up memories of Huysmans's *Là-Bas.* Finally, Tournier does share with the decadents the notion that a conscious violation of a Christian dictum can serve as a paradoxical testament of faith: "If I have a taste for blasphemy, it would nevertheless be a proof that I have the faith."[18]

Despite all these similarities, there is an important difference between Tournier and the decadents, and it concerns the precise nature of "the faith." Most important French writers normally associated with decadence, artists like Verlaine, Huysmans, Baudelaire, and even Rimbaud, have made some sort of peace with Roman Catholicism. They have used Catholicism for various aesthetic purposes and then usually managed to die within the fold. Tournier does more than play with the rites and beauty of religion. He evolves a heretical theology that separates him from the church's thinking. This is particularly apparent with regard to the figure of the crucified Christ. When Barbey d'Aurevilly finished reading *A Rebours* he said that all Huysmans could now do was to choose between the muzzle of a pistol and the foot of the Cross. Huysmans opted for the Cross, but it is this image of the crucified Christ that best exemplifies for Tournier how the church has gone wrong: "Horror of the flesh places the crucifix—a decaying carcass nailed onto two beams—at the center of Catholicism" (*VP,* 62). In *Les Météores* Paul Surin contrasts the serenity of Buddha with the agony of Jesus whose gesture on the Cross is "filled with cries, tears, and contortions" (*M,* 454). He goes on to note that Oriental families like having their pictures taken before the status of Buddha, but "who would dream of being photographed at the foot of the Cross?" (*M,* 454). For Tournier the Cross, unlike Thomas Koussek's Spirit, celebrates death and the denial of what the world offers. What he much prefers in Christianity are the doctrines that reflect life's triumph over death: "the transfiguration on Mt. Thabor and the Resurrection are much more significant than the Cross."[19]

Tournier also distances himself from the church's practice: "The church . . . serving only the institution of bourgeois society and claiming to teach the Gospels while in fact teaching the opposite . . . the church teaches respect for property, hatred of the flesh, and respect for existing power (the Gospel despises money, loves the flesh, and is revolutionary). We are approaching the only solution . . . a church restricted to true Christians. Instead of ten million Catholics in France, there will perhaps only be fifty thousand true Christians."[20]

The revolutionary, flesh-loving Christian church that Tournier envisions is not a decadent fantasy and does not have its seat in Rome. As an institution it exists nowhere and perhaps never will, since its text, the Bible and especially the Gospels, has too radical a message. No institution, no hierarchy or power structure could be comfortable with it. Francis of Assisi discovered that centuries ago when he first tried to have his new order chartered from Rome. Michel Tournier is no Francis of Assisi, but he does share the saint's tradition-shattering belief that the Good News of the Gospel was intended not to alter people's concept of heaven, but to enhance their love for the earth.

Chapter Seven

Conclusion

Tournier and His Lineage

The author Michel Tournier most resembles is Gustave Flaubert. Apart from some personal affinities (a tendency to reclusion, dislike of Paris, an interest in distant lands), both writers are fascinated by the exotic and the erotic, and share an ambivalent attitude toward romanticism. It is the latter quality, this ambivalence toward romanticism, that is by far the most important similarity.

In *Le Vent Paraclet* Tournier maintained that romanticism was the gravedigger of wisdom (*VP,* 275), and in *Madame Bovary* Flaubert provided the specific cause of wisdom's demise. Emma, he says, "had always to get a personal profit from things; she rejected as useless everything that did not contribute immediately to her heart—being by temperament more sentimental than artistic, and looking for emotions, not landscapes."[1] When Emma looked at the world around her she was not interested in discovering what was really there; she sought things that would engender some predetermined feeling. She expected nature to reflect and enhance her state of mind. This is, of course, a version of the pathetic fallacy, one of the staples of romanticism. Another variation of the pathetic fallacy appears in *L'Education sentimentale.* For over thirty years Frédéric Moreau pursues the love of his life, Mme Arnoux. During this period he manages to misunderstand some of the most important events in nineteenth-century French and European history. At the novel's end he realizes that Mme Arnoux was not what he thought she was and that he had indeed wasted the finest years of his life. Frédéric Moreau is something of a fool, and the same can be said for Emma as well.

For Flaubert, however, they are not just fools. While sad

and misguided they certainly are, both Emma and Frédéric were characters dissatisfied with their lives and the all too predictable destinies that lay before them. They wanted something more vital and exciting; their error was not in wanting something different, but in believing that what they sought existed somewhere other than in their own imaginings. Until the very end, if then, they did not understand that they were victims of their own fantasies, and while they both failed to achieve their goals, their quest was not without its joys.

The heroes of Tournier's trilogy (Robinson, Abel, and Paul Surin) are avatars of romanticism. They discover in the world around them exactly what they intended to find. Experience provides them with nothing other than a confirmation of what they believe they already know. Tournier pursues this notion more rigorously and obsessively than does Flaubert; he shows the good (Robinson) and the bad (Paul and Abel) aspects of his characters' fantasies, but any elements of moral judgment constantly yield to the fascination created by the pursuit of illusion. Tournier's heroes, like Flaubert, derive their dynamism from the self-delusions that govern their lives. If then romanticism does in some sense lead to the death of wisdom, wisdom's loss is never entirely lamented.

The characters in *Gaspard, Melchior et Balthazar,* like Flaubert's St. Antoine, may struggle through illusions, but their goal, and one they achieve, is truth. On a philosophical level this is certainly interesting, and in Tournier's case it represents a new direction in his work, but as literature it is less compelling. *La Tentation de Saint Antoine (The Temptation of Saint Anthony),* for all its qualities, never equaled *Madame Bovary* or *L'Education sentimentale.* Similarly, no vision in *Gaspard, Melchior et Balthazar,* no matter how beautific, rivals in fascination the delusions of Robinson, Paul, and Abel. With specific regard to Tournier's novel, *Gaspard, Melchior et Balthazar* may charmingly evoke and then reinterpret a myth that is part of the Judeo-Christian heritage, but except as a memory, it is difficult to assess how much of this heritage has survived the wasteland of the twentieth century. It must be said, however, that one of Tournier's greatest talents is his ability to astonish, and perhaps the gifts of the Magi are only a foretaste of still greater orderings of experience to come.

Tournier Today

In the 28 April 1983 issue of the *New York Review of Books* Roger Shattuck wrote an essay that decried the fact that Michel Tournier "remains virtually unknown in the United States."[2] He offers several reasons to explain this situation. Half-jokingly he suggests there is a conspiracy afoot in academic circles to maintain the dominance of "le nouveau roman" as the official French contemporary novel form. This results in writers who are not in the tradition of Alain Robbe-Grillet and the theorist Roland Barthes being confined to some sort of literary limbo.

While it is certainly true that Tournier's novels are too lacking in stylistic complexity for some scholarly tastes, and that he defies simple classification (a colleague once asked me what "school" Tournier belonged to and then recoiled in horror when I shamefacedly admitted that he did not belong to any), it would be ascribing too much importance to academic influence on readers' tastes to insist (as Shattuck does not) that a cabal of French teachers is to blame. A simpler explanation for Tournier's neglect is that all his works have not yet been translated and the translation of what is arguably his greatest novel, *Le Roi des Aulnes,* has only recently returned to print (New York: Pantheon, 1984).

Shattuck is more serious when he notes that Tournier has some powerful detractors in France who object to what they take to be the author's disquieting fascination with perversion and fascism.[3] One hopes that this study has at the very least put these themes in a more intelligible context. Tournier is obviously quite interested in expanding people's awareness of the complexity of sexual identity and expression. However, in sexual matters he is not the "incorrigible pedagogue."[4] that Shattuck discovers in other areas. Although Tournier describes types of sexual activity that deviate from the norm, he never champions one form over another. In *Les Météores* Alexandre Surin's contempt for heterosexuals has considerable justification, and it quickly becomes apparent that Paul Surin's claims of superiority in sexual expression has no real basis in fact. If Abel Tiffauges is a "bad" person it is not because of "la phorie," but due to his refusal to accept "la phorie" for the innocent instinct that it is.

It is understandable that a reader of *Le Roi des Aulnes* might initially conclude that the novel is a paean to fascism. Nevertheless, a more careful reading, one that allows for Tournier's ironic gifts and one that appreciates the ample evidence of Abel's self-delusion, will soon reveal the novel's true intentions. It is odd that readers who will tolerate and enjoy the tremendous stylistic complexities of the *nouveaux romanciers* will balk at the intellectual complexities of a writer like Tournier.

The basis for Tournier's appeal in Europe, and eventually in the United States, is that he articulates and then explores an attitude about life that finds many echoes among contemporary readers. To use his own terminology, Tournier is intellectually a *sécondaire,* a person deeply pessimistic about what passes for progress, social justice, and happy human relationships. He has experienced white laughter ("le rire blanc"), that sense of life's total meaninglessness. Yet if that were all Tournier had to offer he would not be read as he is today, since neither he nor any other author has explored this landscape of despair with the depth and precision of Céline. What Tournier does is add another element to this grim scenario. He is also a *primaire.*

Despite all that has gone wrong in this century, and despite the fear that things may not improve, Tournier's novels do reflect an enormous sense of the wonder of human existence. His characters, even given the mistaken directions they choose to follow, are attempting to profit from the potential for happiness life contains. The intellect may tell one thing, but that is only a portion of a person's being, and Tournier is constantly demonstrating that the desire for *jouissance* is always more powerful than the numerous calculations which indicate that it will never be achieved. It is the ability to express in his novels this totally contradictory viewpoint, life's meaninglessness and life's splendor, and then chronicle people's struggle to be happy in such an impossible situation, which strikes a very contemporary chord.

Toward the end of *Des Clés et des serrures* Tournier explains what he would like inscribed on his tombstone: "I adore you, you have given me back a hundredfold. Thank you, Life."[5] For a man whose instincts of a *primaire* are constantly challenged by his intellect of a *sécondaire,* this affirmation bespeaks a large amount of courage.

Notes and References

Preface

1. Raymond Sokolov, "Junket of the Year: Les Intellos," *Wall Street Journal,* 15 February 1983, 32.

Chapter One

1. *Le Vent Paraclet* (Paris, 1977), 9; hereafter cited in the text as *VP*.
2. *Le Vol du vampire* (Paris, 1981), 31; hereafter cited in the text as *V*.
3. *Nouvelles littéraires,* no. 2761, 1980, 36.
4. "Dix-huit questions à Michel Tournier," *Dossier,* 1980, 11; this is an interview conducted by Jean-Jacques Brochier.
5. "Michel Tournier," *Le Gai-Pied,* February 1981, 13; this is an interview.
6. "Un écrivain émerveillé," *Entretien* (27 October–12 November 1979), 47; this is an interview with Alain Poirson.
7. Interviewed by R. Vrigny on France-Culture, 11 November 1980. This interview was transcribed from the radio by Editions Gallimard and obtained from their archives. Subsequent references to unpaginated interviews are from this source.
8. "La parole à Michel Tournier: 'De l'or, de la myrrhe et de l'encens,'" *Figaro,* 9 February 1981.
9. "Michel Tournier ou le rire de dieu," *Clair obscur,* 1982, 6.
10. *Les Roi des Aulnes* (Paris, 1970), 11; hereafter cited in the text as *R*.
11. J.-J. Rousseau, *Emile* (Paris: Garnier-Flammarion, 1966), 113.

Chapter Two

1. Rousseau, *Emile,* 238.
2. Ibid., 239.
3. *Vendredi, ou les limbes du Pacifique* (Paris 1967), 7; hereafter cited in the text as *Ve*.
4. See Ian Watt, *The Rise of the Novel* (Berkeley: University of California Press, 1964), 60–93.

5. See Denis Diderot, *Le Fils naturel* (Paris: Nouveaux Classiques Larousse, 1970), 82.

6. John Berger, "Why Look at Animals?" in *About Looking* (New York: Pantheon, 1980), 1–27.

7. S. Freud, "Three Essays on Sexuality," in *Works,* ed. James Strachey (London: Hogarth Press, 1953), 7: 191, 231, 234, 239, 277.

8. Interview on France-Culture, 7 May 1973; the interviewer was not identified.

9. See *Larousse World Mythology.* ed. Pierre Grimal (London: Hamyln, 1973), 118–19.

10. Gilles Deleuze, "Michel Tournier et le monde sans autrui," in *Logique du sens* (Paris, 1969), 352.

11. Interview with Jean-François Josselin in *Le Nouvel Observateur,* 6 December 1971, 57.

12. Ibid., 57.

13. *Vendredi, ou la Vie sauvage* (Paris, 1977), 38; hereafter cited in the text as *VS.*

14. France-Culture, 7 May 1973 (radio interview).

15. *Elle,* 5 November 1973, 96.

16. *Le Nouvel Observateur,* 6 December 1971, 57.

17. Ibid.

18. Ibid.

19. Ibid.

Chapter Three

1. Saul Friedländer, *Reflets du Nazisme* (Paris: Editions du Seuil, 1982), 75.

2. Ibid., 80.

3. Ibid., 100.

4. Ibid., 14, n.

5. K. R. Eissler, *Goethe,* vol. 2 (Detroit: Wayne State University, 1963), 780ff.

6. Rudolf Magnus, *Goethe as a Scientist* (New York: Henry Schuman, 1949), 27.

7. Ibid., 28.

8. Ibid., 110.

9. Ibid., 103.

10. Ibid., 104.

11. Goethe, *Faust,* ed. R.-M. Heffner, H. Rehder, and W. Twaddell, (Madison: University of Wisconsin Press, 1975), 1:57.

12. Ibid., 230; my italics.

13. Michel Bataille, *Gilles de Rais* (Paris: Mercure de France, 1972), 189.

14. *Contes de Perrault,* ed. G. Rouger (Paris: Garnier, 1967), 120.
15. Bataille, *Gilles de Rais,* 81.
16. Georges Bataille, *Le Procès de Gilles de Rais* (Paris: Pauvert, 1972), 57.
17. Ibid., 184.
18. Ibid., 230.
19. Gilles Deleuze and Felix Guattari, *L'Anti-Oedipe, Capitalisme et schizophrénie* (Paris: Editions de Minuit, 1972), 173.
20. Ibid., 174.
21. Ibid., 179.

Chapter Four

1. Robert Kanters, "Creux et plein d'ordures," *Figaro littéraire* 1507 (5 April 1975): 15.
2. Ibid., 17.
3. Angela Huth, "Gemini," *Listener,* 24 November 1981, 14.
4. Not everyone would agree with this viewpoint: "Alexandre . . . is only an esthete; he represents . . . in relation to Paul, the true poet, what Swann or Charles represent in *Remembrance of Time Past* with regard to the narrator" (Jacques Charbot, "Un frère jumeau du monde: Michel Tournier," *Etudes,* July 1976, 58).
5. This is the only Tournier novel where shifting foci can cause difficulty for the reader.
6. *Les Météores* (Paris, 1975), 152; hereafter cited in the text as *M.*
7. This theory will be important in the chapter on *Gaspard, Melchior et Balthazar.*

Chapter Five

1. Interview with Pierre Macaigne in *Le Republicain Lorrain,* 11 June 1978, 32.
2. Interview in *Bulletin de l'Académie royale de langue et de littérature françaises* (Brussels) 56, no. 34 (1978): 307.
3. *Le Coq de bruyère* (Paris, 1978), 16; hereafter cited in the text as *C.*

Chapter Six

1. "Michel Tournier: Je me suis toujours voulu écrivain croyant," *La Croix,* 10 November 1980, 8.
2. The *imprimatur* ("let it be printed") was a license granted by the church to assure readers that the volume contained nothing that was heresy. The practice of granting of an *imprimatur* has been discontinued by the church in recent years.

3. "Michel Tournier: 'J'ai pris ma plume et j'ai inventé la vérité,' " *Journal de Genève,* 9 January 1981, 13; interview with Roger d'Ivernois.

4. Radio interview on France-Culture, 11 November, 1980.

5. Quoted by Nicole Boulanger, "L'Evangile selon Saint-Tournier," *Le Nouvel Observateur,* 1 December 1980.

6. "La parole à Michel Tournier," *Le Nouvel Observateur,* 6 February 1981.

7. Aristotle, *Meteorologica,* trans. H. D. P. Lee (Cambridge: Harvard University Press, 1962), 4.

8. "Michel Tournier: Je me suis . . .," 8.

9. *Gaspard, Melchior et Balthazar* (Paris, 1980), 265; hereafter cited in the text as *G.*

10. "Tournier répond aux critiques: *Les Météores,* chef d'oeuvre ou provocation?" *Figaro littéraire,* 19 December 1975, 15.

11. Interview with Jean-Marie Rouart: "Je me réclame du naturalisme mystique," *Le Quotidien de Paris,* 1982, 28.

12. Alain Poirson, "Une logique contre vents et marées: Entretien avec Michel Tournier," *La Nouvelle Critique,* June–July 1977, 46.

13. "Tournier répond aux critiques," 15.

14. *Nouvelles littéraires,* no. 2761, 1980, 36.

15. Interview with Yvonne Chauffin in *Le Pélérin,* 21 December 1980.

16. Radio interview on France-Culture, 27 November 1980.

17. *Des Clés et des serrures* (Paris, 1979), 8.

18. "Tournier répond aux critiques," 15.

19. "Michel Tournier: Je me suis . . .," 8.

20. Penny Hueston, "An Interview with Michel Tournier," *Meanjin* 38 (May 1978): 404.

Chapter Seven

1. Gustave Flaubert, *Madame Bovary* (Paris: Garnier, 1961), 34; my translation.

2. Roger Shattuck, "Why Not the Best," *New York Review of Books,* 28 April 1983, 8.

3. Ibid., 13–14.

4. Ibid., 13.

5. Quoted by Nicole Boulanger, "L'Evangile selon Saint-Tournier," *Le Nouvel Observateur,* 1 December 1980.

Selected Bibliography

PRIMARY SOURCES

1. Novels
Vendredi, ou les limbes du Pacifique. Paris: Gallimard, 1967.
Le Roi des Aulnes. Paris: Gallimard, 1970.
Les Météores. Paris: Gallimard, 1975.
Gaspard, Melchior et Balthazar. Paris: Gallimard, 1980.

2. Essays
Le Vent Paraclet. Paris: Gallimard, 1977.
Le Vol du vampire. Paris: Mercure de France, 1981.

3. Collected Short Works
Le Coq de Bruyère. Paris: Gallimard, 1978.

4. For Children
Vendredi ou la Vie sauvage. Paris: Gallimard, 1977.
Pierrot ou les Secrets de la nuit. Illustrated by Danièle Bour. Paris: Gallimard, 1979.
Barbedor. Paris: Gallimard, 1980.

5. Introductions by Tournier
Aventures et secrets du collectionneur, by Laurent Gouvion Saint-Cyr. Paris: Stock, 1971.
Des Clés et les serrures. Paris: Chêne/Hachette, 1979. A collection of photographs chosen and commented on by Tournier.
La Famille des enfants. Paris: Flammarion, 1977.
Mers, Plages, Sources et Torrents, Arbes, by Lucien Clergue. Paris: Editions Perceval, n.d.
Morts et résurrections de Dieter Appelt. Berlin: Herscher, 1981.
Venise, hier et demain, by Fulvio Roiter. Paris: Chêne/Hachette, 1973.

6. English Translations
Friday and Robinson: Life on Speranza Island. Translated by Ralph Mannheim. New York: Knopf, 1972. Illustrated edition for grades 7 and up. Translation of *Vendredi, ou la vie sauvage.*

Friday, or the Other Island. Translated by Norman Denny. London:
  Collins, 1969; New York, Doubleday, 1969. Translation of *Ven-*
  dredi, ou les limbes du Pacifique.
The Four Wise Men. Translated by Ralph Mannheim. New York: Dou-
  bleday, 1982. Translation of *Gaspard, Melchior et Balthazar.*
Gemini. Translated by Ann Carter. London: Collins, 1981; New York:
  Doubleday, 1981. Translation of *Les Météores.*
The Ogre. Translated by Barbara Bray. London: Collins, 1972; New
  York: Doubleday, 1972. Translation of *Le Roi des Aulnes.*

7. Interviews

Brochier, Jean-Jacques. "Qu'est-ce que c'est la littérature? Un entretien
  avec Michel Tournier." *Magazine littéraire,* no. 179 (1982):80–
  86. Tournier presents his views on other French writers.
Brun, Jany. "Michel Tournier." *Artistes et Variétés,* 352 (December
  1979):7–8. Tournier discusses his musical interests.
Chancel, Jacques. "Michel Tournier: 'Le secret d'un livre est la pa-
  tience.' " *Figaro-Dimanche* (9 December 1979):29. Tournier explains how he likes to live and discusses his interest in
  photography.
Hueston, Penny. "An Interview with Michel Tournier." *Meanjin* 38
  (May 1978):401–8. Tournier's only interview in an English-lan-
  guage journal. Helpful for his views on religion.
d'Ivernois, Roger, "Michel Tournier: 'J'ai pris ma plume et j'ai inventé
  la vérité.' " *Journal de Genève,* 9 January 1981, 13. Tournier discusses religion.
de Montremy, J. M. "Michel Tournier: Je me suis toujours voulu
  écrivain croyant." *La Croix,* 10 November 1980, 8. Tournier
  discusses his religious beliefs.

SECONDARY SOURCES

Amery, Jean. "Asthetizismus der Barbarei: Uber Tourniers Roman
  Der Erlkönig." *Merkur* 28 (1973):73–79. Bitter attack on what
  the author takes to be Nazi elements in *Le Roi des Aulnes.*
Bougnoux, Daniel. "Des Metaphores à la phorie." *Critique* 28
  (1972):527–43. An analysis of the psychological ramifications of
  "la phorie."
Cloonan, William. "The Artist Conscious and Unconscious in *Le*
  Roi des Aulnes." *Kentucky Romance Quarterly* 29, no. 2 (1982):191–
  200.

Deleuze, Gilles. "Michel Tournier et le monde sans autrui." In *Logique du sens.* Paris: Editions de Minuit, 1969. Intelligent discussion of the island's role and the complexity of sexual identity in *Vendredi.*

Friedländer, Saul. *Reflets du nazisme.* Paris: Seuil, 1982. Fine discussion of upsurge of interest in nazism. Particularly valuable with regard to *Le Roi des Aulnes.*

Fumaroli, Marc. "Michel Tournier et l'esprit d'enfance." *Commentaire* 3, no. 12 (1980–82):638–43. Tournier compared to Anatole France and to French classicism.

Purdy, Anthony. *"Les Météores* de Michel Tournier: une perspective hétérologique." *Littérature* 40 (1980):32–43. An analysis of *Les Météores* founded on philosophical/psychological approach developed by Georges Bataille.

Sud (1980). A special issue of this journal is devoted to Tournier. The issue lists no editor or volume number. It is cataloged in the Bibliotheque National under the rubric of "Special Issues."

Index